→ *Program Authors* ←

Carl Bereiter, Ph.D.

Sandra N. Kaplan, Ed.D.

Michael Pressley, Ph.D.

A Division of The McGraw·Hill Companies

Columbus, Ohio

☀ Acknowledgments ☀

Grateful acknowledgment is given to the following publishers and copyright owners for permissions granted to reprint selections from their publications. All possible care has been taken to trace ownership and secure permission for each selection included. In case of any errors or omissions, the Publisher will be pleased to make suitable acknowledgments in future editions.

FRIENDSHIP
"The Shepherd and the Wild Goats" from AESOP'S FABLES Copyright © 2001 by Jerry Pinkney. Used by permission of SeaStar Books, a division of North-South Books, Inc., New York.

From THE GOLDEN STAG AND OTHER FOLK TALES FROM INDIA by Isabel Wyatt, copyright © 1962 and renewed 1990 David McKay Company, Inc. Used by permission of David McKay Company, a division of Random House, Inc.

Excerpt from THE LITTLE PRINCE, copyright 1943 by Harcourt, Inc., copyright renewed 1971 by Consuelo de Saint-Exupéry, English translation copyright © 2000 by Richard Howard, reprinted by permission of Harcourt, Inc.
From THE LITTLE PRINCE © Gallimard 1944. First English Edition published in 1945 by William Heinemann Ltd and used with permission of Egmont Books Limited, London

CITY WILDLIFE
THE PIED PIPER. Illustrations © David Wenzel, used by permission of Worthington Press, a subsidiary of Oxford Resources, Inc.

"Chester" from THE CRICKET IN TIMES SQUARE by George Selden, illustrated by Garth Williams. Copyright © 1960 by George Selden Thompson and Garth Williams.

Copyright renewed 1988 by George Selden Thompson. Reprinted by permission of Farrar, Straus and Giroux, LLC.

FLY HIGH FLY LOW from CORDUROY & COMPANY: A DON FREEMAN TREASURY. Reprinted with permission of the estate of Don and Lydia Freeman.

IMAGINATION
"Most Beds" from THE BED BOOK by Sylvia Plath. TEXT COPYRIGHT © 1976 BY TED HUGHES. Illustrations by Emily Arnold McCully. Used by permission of HarperCollins Publishers.

MANY MOONS, copyright © 1943 by James Thurber, © renewed 1960 by Helen Thurber, reprinted with permission of Harcourt, Inc.

MONEY
A CHAIR FOR MY MOTHER by VERA B. WILLIAMS. COPYRIGHT © 1982 BY VERA B. WILLIAMS. GREENWILLOW BOOKS. Used by permission of HarperCollins Publishers.

"Henry Gets Rich" from HENRY AND BEEZUS by BEVERLY CLEARY. TEXT COPYRIGHT © 1952 BY BEVERLY CLEARY. Used by permission of HarperCollins Publishers.

STORYTELLING
From MY INDIAN BOYHOOD by Chief Luther Standing Bear. Copyright 1931 by Chief Luther Standing Bear, renewed © 1959 by Mary M. Jones. Reprinted by Houghton Mifflin Company. All rights reserved.

"The Pink Stationery" from BETSY AND TACY GO DOWNTOWN by Maud Hart Lovelace. Used by permission.

COUNTRY LIFE
"Journey for Meadow Boots" from MIRACLES ON MAPLE HILL, copyright © 1956 by Virginia Sorensen and renewed 1984 by Virginia Sorensen Waugh reprinted by permission of Harcourt, Inc.

Copyright © 1956 by Virginia Sorensen. Excerpt from MIRACLES ON MAPLE HILL, published by Harcourt Brace and Company. Reprinted by permission of Curtis Brown, Ltd.

From THE COUNTRY ARTIST: A STORY ABOUT BEATRIX POTTER by David R. Collins. Copyright 1989 by Carolrhoda Books, Inc. A Division of Lerner Publishing Group. Used by permission of the publisher. All rights reserved.

All images reproduced by kind permission of Frederick Warne & Co. 3 illustrations from THE TALE OF PETER RABBIT by Beatrix Potter. Copyright © Frederick Warne & Co., 1902, 2002. 2 illustrations from THE TALE OF SAMUEL WHISKERS by Beatrix Potter. Copyright © Frederick Warne & Co., 1908, 2002. 1 illustration from THE TALE OF PIGLING BLAND by Beatrix Potter. Copyright © Frederick Warne & Co., 1913, 2002. 1 illustration from THE TALE OF JEMIMA PUDDLE-DUCK by Beatrix Potter. Copyright © Frederick Warne & Co., 1908, 2002. 1 illustration from THE TALE OF TOM KITTEN by Beatrix Potter. Copyright © Frederick Warne & Co., 1907, 2002. 1 illustration from THE TALE OF THE FLOPSY BUNNIES by Beatrix Potter. Copyright © Frederick Warne & Co., 1909, 2002. 1 illustration from THE TALE OF MR. JEREMY FISHER by Beatrix Potter. Copyright © Frederick Warne & Co., 1906, 2002.

"Holding Down A Claim" from THESE HAPPY GOLDEN YEARS by Laura Ingalls Wilder. TEXT COPYRIGHT 1943 BY LAURA INGALLS WILDER. COPYRIGHT RENEWED 1971 BY ROGER LEA MACBRIDE. ILLUSTRATIONS COPYRIGHT 1953 BY GARTH WILLIAMS. COPYRIGHT © RENEWED 1981 BY GARTH WILLIAMS. Used by permission of HarperCollins Publishers.

www.sra4kids.com

SRA/McGraw-Hill

A Division of The McGraw·Hill Companies

Send all inquiries to:
SRA/McGraw-Hill
8787 Orion Place
Columbus, OH 43240-4027

Printed in the United States of America.

ISBN 0-07-572488-X

3 4 5 6 7 8 9 QWV 07 06 05

◆ *Level 3* ◆

Friendship

◆

City Wildlife

◆

Imagination

◆

Money

◆

Storytelling

◆

Country Life

Table of Contents

UNIT 1 Friendship

UNIT 2 City Wildlife

UNIT 3 Imagination

UNIT 4 Money

UNIT 5 Storytelling

UNIT 6 Country Life

Friendship

A friend is a gift you give yourself.
—Robert Louis Stevenson—

The Shepherd and the Wild Goats

from *Aesop's Fables*

retold and illustrated by Jerry Pinkney

A shepherd was out with his goats on a mountainside when a fierce storm blew in. He drove the animals into a nearby cave for shelter, and found that a flock of wild goats had taken refuge there as well.

"If I feed these wild goats," thought the shepherd, "then perhaps they'll stay with me. In no time at all my flock will double in size!"

So the shepherd gave the wild goats the best of his grain and hay, and made sure they had fresh water to drink. But since he had only a little food with him, he gave his own goats no more than a few handfuls of grain.

When the storm finally passed, the wild goats bounded out of the cave without a backward glance. "Wait!" cried the shepherd angrily. "Is this the thanks I get for taking care of you?"

One of the wild goats looked back. "We saw how you treated your own flock," she answered. "Why should we think you'd treat us any differently if we stayed with you?"

Don't neglect old friends for new ones.

About the Author and Illustrator

Jerry Pinkney was born in 1939 in Philadelphia, Pennsylvania. At an early age he showed a talent for drawing, and his family encouraged him to develop his gift. Mr. Pinkney began publishing children's books in the 1960s. The books often portray African and African American characters. His books have won prestigious prizes, including Caldecott Honors and Coretta Scott King Awards. Mr. Pinkney's artwork has been featured in museums across the United States.

The Three Friends

from *The Golden Stag
and Other Folk Tales from India*
by Isabel Wyatt
illustrated by Ruth Araceli

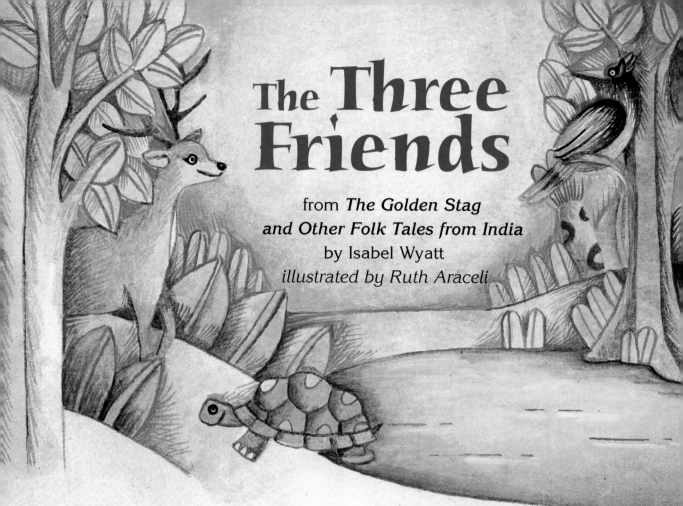

A deer had his lair near a lake in a wood. In a tree on the bank of this lake, a woodpecker had her nest. In the mud at the edge of the lake, a turtle had his mud bath.

The three were fast friends.

One day, a hunter came that way. He saw the footprints of the deer that went down from the wood to the lake; and in the deer's track he set a trap of strong leather thongs.

At dusk, the deer went down to the lake to drink. He trod on the trap, and the leather thongs held his foot. He cried the cry of capture:

"Friends! Friends! I am fast in a snare!"

The woodpecker flew down from her treetop. The turtle rose up out of his mud bath. They came to the help of the deer.

"My teeth are sharp," said the turtle. "I can bite the leather thongs."

All night he bit with his sharp teeth at the strong leather thongs. When dawn came, the turtle said, "I have cut Deer free from all the thongs but two. The hunter will soon be here. I need more time."

"I will go and try to keep the hunter back," said the woodpecker.

And off she flew to the hut of the hunter.

Soon she saw the front door open, and out came the hunter, his knife in his hand.

The woodpecker gave a shrill cry, flew at his face, and struck at him with her beak and her wings.

"I must go back," said the hunter. "I shall have bad luck if I go on now."

So he went back into his hut and lay down and slept again.

Then he got up, and took his knife.

"This time I will go out by the back door," he said, "so that I do not meet bad luck again."

So out he went by the back door.

But again the woodpecker gave a shrill cry, flew at his face, and struck at him with her beak and her wings.

"I must go back," said the hunter again. "I shall have bad luck if I go on now."

So again he went back into his hut, and lay down and slept.

This time, when he got up, he took his bow as well as his knife.

"If I meet bad luck this time," he said, "I will stab it or I will shoot it."

When the woodpecker saw the bow and the knife, she flew to her friends.

"The hunter is on his way!" she cried out to them.

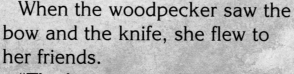

The turtle had cut the deer's foot free from all the thongs but one. Blood was on his mouth. He grew weak; but still he bit at the last thong of leather.

The deer saw the hunter stride out of the wood, his knife and his bow in his hand. In his fear, he burst the last thong of the snare and fled into the wood.

The woodpecker flew to her treetop. But the turtle was so weak that he just lay still on the grass.

"I have lost the deer," said the hunter, "but at least I will have the turtle."

And he took him up, thrust him into a bag, and tied the bag up tight.

The deer saw all this. "Now I must do for Turtle what Turtle did for me," he said.

So he let the hunter see him, then took slow steps, as if he were lame and weak. The hunter hung his bag on the woodpecker's tree, and went after the deer, his bow and his knife in his hands.

The deer led him deep into the wood.

Then down flew the woodpecker, to peck a hole in the hunter's bag.

"Turtle, pop out your head!" she cried. "Jump down to the grass!"

The turtle put out his head. "It is too far," he said. "I shall smash my shell to bits."

But as soon as the hunter was deep in the wood, the deer ran back, as swift as the wind. With his long horns he slid the bag down from the tree to the grass; and out crept the turtle by the hole the woodpecker had made.

18

When the hunter came back, all he saw was his torn bag on the grass. The deer had run, the woodpecker had flown, and the turtle had swum, to the far side of the lake.

Here the deer soon had a new lair, the woodpecker a new nest, and the turtle a new mud bath.

And all three were still fast friends.

In The Little Prince, *a pilot crash-landed in the Sahara and came across a little prince. The little prince came from a tiny planet that he shared with a vain rose. The rose's demands caused the little prince unhappiness, and he decided to leave home. While the pilot attempted to fix his plane, the little prince asked questions, made observations, and told stories. One story he told was about a wise fox he met on Earth.*

The Fox's Secret

from *The Little Prince*

written and illustrated by Antoine de Saint-Exupéry
translated from the French by Richard Howard

"Good morning," said the fox.

"Good morning," the little prince answered politely, though when he turned around he saw nothing.

"I'm here," the voice said, "under the apple tree."

"Who are you?" the little prince asked. "You're very pretty . . ."

"I'm a fox," the fox said.

"Come and play with me," the little prince proposed. "I'm feeling so sad."

"I can't play with you," the fox said. "I'm not tamed."

"Ah! Excuse me," said the little prince. But upon reflection he added, "What does *tamed* mean?"

"You're not from around here," the fox said. "What are you looking for?"

"I'm looking for people," said the little prince. "What does *tamed* mean?"

"People," said the fox, "have guns and they hunt. It's quite troublesome. And they also raise chickens. That's the only interesting thing about them. Are you looking for chickens?"

"No," said the little prince, "I'm looking for friends. What does *tamed* mean?"

"It's something that's been too often neglected. It means 'to create ties' . . ."

"'To create ties'?"

"That's right," the fox said. "For me you're only a little boy just like a hundred thousand other little boys. And I have no need of you. And you have no need of me, either. For you I'm only a fox like a hundred thousand other foxes. But if you tame me, we'll need each other. You'll be the only boy in the world for me. I'll be the only fox in the world for you . . ."

"I'm beginning to understand," the little prince said. "There's a flower . . . I think she's tamed me . . ."

"Possibly," the fox said. "On Earth, one sees all kinds of things."

"Oh, this isn't on Earth," the little prince said.

The fox seemed quite intrigued. "On another planet?"

"Yes."

"Are there hunters on that planet?"

"No."

"Now that's interesting. And chickens?"

"No."

"Nothing's perfect," sighed the fox. But he returned to his idea. "My life is monotonous. I hunt chickens; people hunt me. All chickens are just alike, and all men are just alike. So I'm rather bored. But if you tame me, my life will be filled with sunshine.

I'll know the sound of footsteps that will be different from all the rest. Other footsteps send me back underground. Yours will call me out of my burrow like music. And then, look! You see the wheat fields over there? I don't eat bread. For me wheat is of no use whatever. Wheat fields say nothing to me. Which is sad.

But you have hair the color of gold. So it will be wonderful, once you've tamed me! The wheat, which is golden, will remind me of you. And I'll love the sound of the wind in the wheat . . ."

The fox fell silent and stared at the little prince for a long while. "Please . . . tame me!" he said.

"I'd like to," the little prince replied, "but I haven't much time. I have friends to find and so many things to learn."

"The only things you learn are the things you tame," said the fox. "People haven't time to learn anything. They buy things ready-made in stores. But since there are no stores where you can buy friends, people no longer have friends. If you want a friend, tame me!"

"What do I have to do?" asked the little prince.

"You have to be very patient," the fox answered. "First you'll sit down a little ways away from me, over there, in the grass. I'll watch you out of the corner of my eye, and you won't say anything. Language is the source of misunderstandings. But day by day, you'll be able to sit a little closer . . ."

The next day the little prince returned.

"It would have been better to return at the same time," the fox said. "For instance, if you come at four in the afternoon, I'll begin to be happy by three. The closer it gets to four, the happier I'll feel. By four I'll be all excited and worried; I'll discover what it costs to be happy! But if you come at any old time, I'll never know when I should prepare my heart . . . There must be rites."

"What's a *rite?*" asked the little prince.

"That's another thing that's been too often neglected," said the fox. "It's the fact that one day is different from the other days, one hour from the other hours. My hunters, for example, have a rite. They dance with the village girls on Thursdays.

So Thursday's a wonderful day: I can take a
stroll all the way to the vineyards. If the
hunters danced whenever they chose, the days
would all be just alike, and I'd have no holiday
at all."

That was how the little prince tamed the fox.
And when the time to leave was near:
   "Ah!" the fox said. "I shall weep."
   "It's your own fault," the little prince said.
"I never wanted to do you any harm, but you
insisted that I tame you . . ."
   "Yes, of course," the fox said.
   "But you're going to weep!" said the little
prince.
   "Yes, of course," the fox said.
   "Then you get nothing out of it?"
   "I get something," the fox said, "because of
the color of the wheat." Then he added, "Go
look at the roses again. You'll understand that
yours is the only rose in all the world. Then
come back to say good-bye, and I'll make you
the gift of a secret."

The little prince went to look at the roses again.

"You're not at all like my rose. You're nothing at all yet," he told them. "No one has tamed you and you haven't tamed anyone. You're the way my fox was. He was just a fox like a hundred thousand others. But I've made him my friend, and now he's the only fox in all the world."

And the roses were humbled.

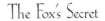

"You're lovely, but you're empty," he went on. "One couldn't die for you. Of course, an ordinary passerby would think my rose looked just like you. But my rose, all on her own, is more important than all of you together, since she's the one I've watered. Since she's the one I put under glass. Since she's the one I sheltered behind a screen. Since she's the one for whom I killed the caterpillars (except the two or three for butterflies). Since she's the one I listened to when she complained, or when she boasted, or even sometimes when she said nothing at all. Since she's *my* rose."

And he went back to the fox.
"Good-bye," he said.
"Good-bye," said the fox. "Here is my secret. It's quite simple: One sees clearly only with the heart. Anything essential is invisible to the eyes."

"Anything essential is invisible to the eyes," the little prince repeated, in order to remember.

"It's the time you spent on your rose that makes your rose so important."

"It's the time I spent on my rose . . . ," the little prince repeated, in order to remember.

"People have forgotten this truth," the fox said. "But you mustn't forget it. You become responsible forever for what you've tamed. You're responsible for your rose . . ."

"I'm responsible for my rose . . . ," the little prince repeated, in order to remember.

About the Author and Illustrator

Antoine de Saint-Exupéry, born on June 29th, 1900, had two passions in his life: flying and writing. Fortunately, he was able to combine these passions in works like *Night Flight, Wind, Sand, and Stars,* and *The Little Prince,* his only book written for children. More than fifty years after its publication, readers still return to this story of a stranded pilot, a special little boy, and the friendship they form out in the desert.

City Wildlife

GOODS

Those who wish to pet and baby wild
animals, "love" them. But those who
respect their natures and wish to let
them live normal lives, love them more.
—Edwin Way Teale—

The Pied Piper of Hameln

a German folktale retold by Carol Ottolenghi

illustrated by David Wenzel

Many years ago, long before the rats came, Hameln was just another crowded German city. Farmers drove their wagons into town to sell vegetables. Boats loaded with timber sailed up and down the Weser River. Peddlers pushed carts through the streets, shouting out, "Fabric for sale! The softest velvet this side of the Weser!" and "Jewelry boxes! The best from Bonn!" Children chased chickens, the chickens dodged carts, and shopkeepers yelled at both children and fowl. Laughter and bustle echoed off the cobblestone streets of Hameln.

Then the rats invaded.

No one knows where the rats came from. Some folks say they came from deep in the forest on Kuppelberg Hill. Others think the rats swam down the river from another town. But that doesn't really matter, because Hameln suddenly was overrun by thousands and thousands of huge, horrible, hungry rats.

The rats were smart and quick. They chewed through the walls of every home in Hameln. They nested in boots and pockets and top hats. They chased cats and dogs, stole bread from the tables, and spread disease wherever they went.

People stopped coming to Hameln. Farmers stayed away because the rats swarmed over their wagons faster than the farmers could unload the food. Boat captains and peddlers moved to other cities. Shopkeepers didn't open their shops because the rats had eaten or ruined everything they had to sell. And in every house children sat for hours, watching the rat holes. They held heavy pans or sticks, ready to "whap" any rat that dared to show a whisker.

The rat invasion became so bad that the town mayor held a meeting to decide if everyone should leave the city. But the rats close by chittered and gnawed so loudly that no one could hear anyone else speak.

Then a high, trilling note sliced through the
noise. One by one, the people of Hameln quit
yelling at their neighbors. They turned and
stared at the stranger with a flute. He was tall,
and so thin that his elbows and knees stuck out
like doorknobs. He had a large, red hat with
a long feather. He wore a red and yellow coat
with a red and yellow scarf. His red shoes
turned up at the ends.

When he entered the mayor's office, the
stranger spoke. "I can get rid of the rats by
tomorrow," he said. "For a price."

Some people laughed at the stranger's foolishness, some were angry, and some folks were confused. The stranger ignored them all. He smiled and hummed softly.

After a few minutes, the mayor of Hameln spoke. "Nonsense! We've tried everything. Cats, dogs, traps—nothing has worked. Hameln is filled with thousands and thousands of rats. What makes you think you can get rid of them?"

"Oh, let's just say that I know what I know. And by tomorrow," the stranger smiled and answered, "they'll all be gone. Listen. Do you hear any rats now?"

The people strained their ears, but the only sounds they heard were shuffling feet and muffled breathing. Neighbors began nudging each other and whispering.

At last the mayor said, "No, I don't, don't hear a one. Very well," he continued, "what is your price to get rid of the rats?"

"One silver penny for each rat."

The Mayor turned pale. "But that will add up to thousands of florins!" he cried.

The Pied Piper answered, "If you do not wish to pay my price, you may keep the rats."

He turned and started walking out of town.

"Wait!" called the mayor. "We will pay you a silver penny for each rat. *After* the rats are gone."

The Pied Piper smiled. "Of course."

He turned to the people, swept his hat from his head, and bowed low.

"Good people of Hameln," he said loudly, "your mayor has agreed to pay me one silver penny for every rat. So all of you must go into your homes. Don't come out until I say it is safe. Watch the parade from your windows and doorways, though, for this very day the rats shall march out of Hameln, and your city will be yours again!"

The crowd started to cheer. The Pied Piper bowed low again, waved his hat, and lifted his flute to his lips.

The Pied Piper walked to the middle of the town square. Suddenly, a shrill note pierced the air. At first, it was the only noise the townspeople heard. Then they heard the scratchy scurrying of many feet, the chittering of many small voices. The scratching and chittering sounds grew until the townspeople had to cover their ears with their hands, pillows, and scarves.

But no one left the windows because outside the most amazing sight was occurring. Rats were squeezing under doors, leaping from roofs, scampering up from cellars, and climbing down the drainpipes. Big rats and little rats, fat rats and thin rats, brown rats, black rats and white rats, every rat in Hameln rushed to where the Pied Piper stood and played.

Then the Pied Piper began to play a marching tune. The rats' little paws kept time. He turned and left the square, and *pat, pat, pat* the rats marched behind him. They reached the Weser River and halted. Still playing the flute with one hand, the Pied Piper waved his hat over the river. A whirlpool began swirling in the middle of the river.

As the piper played faster, the rats jumped into the river and swam to the whirlpool. They were sucked into the frothy water and disappeared forever. The Pied Piper played a few more minutes, then stopped. Slowly he walked back to the square.

The whole town had gathered there. When the people saw the Pied Piper (and not a single rat), they cheered until they were hoarse. The mayor grabbed the piper's hand and shook it happily.

The Pied Piper smiled. "I'll take my money and be off," he said.

The mayor stopped shaking the piper's hand and the crowd quieted.

"Hmmm," said the mayor. "I don't see any rats."

"And you won't," said the piper. "You agreed to pay one silver penny for each rat."

"When I get my rats," said the mayor. "Else how can I count how many there were?"

"What?" cried the Pied Piper. "I can't give them to you. They've all drowned."

"Well," said the mayor, "if I don't get my rats, you don't get your silver. But," he continued, "you did a good job. Here are fifty silver pennies."

He held out a small brown money bag. The Pied Piper turned to the crowd.

"People of Hameln!" he shouted. "If you don't pay me what you promised I shall pipe another tune."

The crowd began to grumble. No one wanted to pay so much money for one night's work.

"The rats are gone," said the mayor. "You can't bring them back. Take what we offer and go."

The piper pushed the money bag away. As he left the square, a young woman stopped him. She held her crippled son's hand in her right hand and a grimy red change-purse in her left.

"Take it," she said, giving him the purse. "It's not much, but it's all I have. You earned it."

The Pied Piper tucked the purse into his pants. Then he raised his flute to his lips again. A sweet, laughing note floated over the square. Music poured over the people like a spring rain.

Clap, clap, clap. The town's children started clapping their hands to the beat. They were so happy that none of the adults thought anything was wrong when the Pied Piper led the children skipping toward Kuppelberg Hill.

The piper waved his hat and a hole opened in the side of the hill, showing a small cave. And wonder of wonders! Inside the mountain was a land where bees had no stings and horses had wings. Carnival music and the smells of cotton candy and fresh-baked cinnamon swirls filled the air.

The adults still in the town square heard the music. They turned and saw the hole in the hill, where no hole had been before. They started to run toward the Pied Piper and their children.

The dancing, singing children followed the piper into the wonderful land. The young crippled boy was the last child to reach the hole. The Pied Piper stopped him. "You can't come with us," the piper said in a kind voice. "Your mother already paid me."

The piper stepped back into the hole and it closed, just as the adults reached it.

After that day, there were no more rats in Hameln. But there were many parents who cried long nights, wishing their children were back home with them. If only they had paid the piper . . .

Chester

from *The Cricket in Times Square*
by George Selden
illustrated by Garth Williams

*One night, Mario Bellini hears a strange sound
while working at his parents' newspaper stand.
He hears a cricket chirping—in the Times Square
subway station! Mario finds Chester Cricket in
the station. He convinces his parents to let him
keep Chester at the stand. Tucker Mouse also lives
in the station. Tucker decides to visit his new
neighbor.*

Tucker Mouse had been
watching the Bellinis and
listening to what they said.
Next to scrounging, eavesdropping
on human beings was what he
enjoyed most. That was one of the
reasons he lived in the Times Square
subway station. As soon as the family
disappeared, he darted out across the
floor and scooted up to the newsstand. At one side
the boards had separated and there was a wide
space he could jump through. He'd been in a few
times before—just exploring. For a moment he
stood under the three legged stool, letting his eyes
get used to the darkness. Then he jumped up on it.

"Psst!" he whispered. "Hey you up there—are you awake?"

There was no answer.

"Psst! Psst! Hey!" Tucker whispered again, louder this time.

From the shelf above came a scuffling, like little feet feeling their way to the edge. "Who is that going 'psst'?" said a voice.

"It's me," said Tucker. "Down here on the stool."

A black head, with two shiny black eyes, peered down at him. "Who are you?"

"A mouse," said Tucker, "Who are *you?*"

"I'm Chester Cricket," said the cricket. He had a high, musical voice. Everything he said seemed to be spoken to an unheard melody.

"My name's Tucker," said Tucker Mouse. "Can I come up?"

"I guess so," said Chester Cricket. "This isn't my house anyway."

Tucker jumped up beside the cricket and looked him all over. "A cricket," he said admiringly. "So you're a cricket. I never saw one before."

"I've seen mice before," the cricket said. "I knew quite a few back in Connecticut."

"Is that where you're from?" asked Tucker.

"Yes," said Chester. "I guess I'll never see it again," he added wistfully.

"How did you get to New York?" asked Tucker Mouse.

"It's a long story," sighed the cricket.

"Tell me," said Tucker, settling back on his haunches. He loved to hear stories. It was almost as much fun as eavesdropping—if the story was true.

"Well it must have been two—no, three days ago," Chester Cricket began. "I was sitting on top of my stump, just enjoying the weather and thinking how nice it was that summer had started. I live inside an old tree stump, next to a willow tree, and I often go up to the roof to look around. And I'd been practicing jumping that day too. On the other side of the stump from the willow tree there's a brook that runs past, and I'd been jumping back and forth across it to get my legs in condition for the summer. I do a lot of jumping, you know."

"Me too," said Tucker Mouse. "Especially around the rush hour."

"And I had just finished jumping when I smelled something," Chester went on, "liverwurst, which I love."

"You like liverwurst?" Tucker broke in. "Wait! Wait! Just wait!"

In one leap, he sprang down all the way from the shelf to the floor and dashed over to his drain pipe. Chester shook his head as he watched him go. He thought Tucker was a very excitable person—even for a mouse.

Inside the drain pipe, Tucker's nest was a jumble of papers, scraps of cloth, buttons, lost jewelry, small change, and everything else that can be picked up in a subway station. Tucker tossed things left and right in a wild search. Neatness was not one of the things he aimed at in life. At last he discovered what he was looking for: a big piece of liverwurst he had found earlier that evening. It was meant to be for breakfast tomorrow, but he decided that meeting his first cricket was a special occasion. Holding the liverwurst between his teeth, he whisked back to the newsstand.

"Look!" he said proudly, dropping the meat in front of Chester Cricket. "Liverwurst! You continue the story—we'll enjoy a snack too."

"That's very nice of you," said Chester. He was touched that a mouse he had known only a few minutes would share his food with him. "I had a little chocolate before, but besides that, nothing for three days."

"Eat! Eat!" said Tucker. He bit the liverwurst into two pieces and gave Chester the bigger one. "So you smelled the liverwurst—then what happened?"

"I hopped down from the stump and went off toward the smell," said Chester.

"Very logical," said Tucker Mouse, munching with his cheeks full. "Exactly what I would have done."

"It was coming from a picnic basket," said Chester. "A couple of tuffets away from my stump the meadow begins, and there was a whole bunch of people having a picnic. They had hard boiled eggs, and cold roast chicken, and roast beef, and a whole lot of other things besides the liverwurst sandwiches, which I smelled."

Tucker Mouse moaned with pleasure at the thought of all that food.

"They were having such a good time laughing and singing songs that they didn't notice me when I jumped into the picnic basket," continued Chester. "I was sure they wouldn't mind if I had just a taste."

"Naturally not," said Tucker Mouse sympathetically. "Why mind? Plenty for all. Who could blame you?"

"Now I have to admit," Chester went on, "I had more than a taste. As a matter of fact, I ate so much that I couldn't keep my eyes open—what with being tired from the jumping and everything. And I fell asleep right there in the picnic basket. The first thing I knew, somebody had put a bag on top of me that had the last of the roast beef sandwiches in it. I couldn't move!"

"Imagine!" Tucker exclaimed. "Trapped under roast beef sandwiches! Well, there are worse fates."

"At first I wasn't too frightened," said Chester. "After all, I thought, they probably come from New Canaan or some other nearby town. They'll have to unpack the basket sooner or later. Little did I know!" He shook his head and sighed. "I could feel the basket being carried into a car and riding somewhere and then being lifted down. That must have been the railroad station. Then I went up again and there was a rattling and roaring sound, the way a train makes. By this time I was pretty scared. I knew every minute was taking me further away from my stump, but there wasn't anything I could do. I was getting awfully cramped too, under those roast beef sandwiches."

"Didn't you try to eat your way out?" asked Tucker.

"I didn't have any room," said Chester. "But every now and then the train would give a lurch and I managed to free myself a little. We traveled on and on, and then the train stopped. I didn't have any idea where we were, but as soon as the basket was carried off, I could tell from the noise it must be New York."

"You never were here before?" Tucker asked.

"Goodness no!" said Chester. "But I've heard about it. There was a swallow I used to know who told about flying over New York every spring and fall on her way to the North and back. But what would I be doing here?" He shifted uneasily from one set of legs to another. "I'm a country cricket."

"Don't worry," said Tucker Mouse. "I'll feed you liverwurst. You'll be all right. Go on with the story."

"It's almost over," said Chester. "The people got off one train and walked a ways and got on another—even noisier than the first."

"Must have been the subway," said Tucker.

"I guess so," Chester Cricket said. "You can imagine how scared I was. I didn't know *where* I was going! For all I knew they could have been heading for Texas, although I don't guess many people from Texas come all the way to Connecticut for a picnic."

"It could happen," said Tucker, nodding his head.

"Anyway I worked furiously to get loose. And finally I made it. When they got off the second train, I took a flying leap and landed in a pile of dirt over in the corner of this place where we are."

"Such an introduction to New York," said Tucker, "to land in a pile of dirt in the Times Square subway station. Tsk, tsk, tsk."

"And here I am," Chester concluded forlornly. "I've been lying over there for three days not knowing what to do. At last I got so nervous I began to chirp."

"That was the sound!" interrupted Tucker Mouse. "I heard it, but I didn't know what it was."

"Yes, that was me," said Chester. "Usually I don't chirp until later on in the summer—but my goodness, I had to do *something!*"

The cricket had been sitting next to the edge of the shelf. For some reason—perhaps it was a faint noise, like padded feet tiptoeing across the floor—he happened to look down. A shadowy form that had been crouching silently below in the darkness made a spring and landed right next to Tucker and Chester.

"Watch out!" Chester shouted, "A cat!" He dove headfirst into the matchbox.

About the Author

George Selden wrote seven books in the Cricket series. *The Cricket in Times Square* is the first in the series and the most popular. Even now, decades later, Chester, Tucker, Harry, and all their friends delight both children and adults.

Fly High Fly Low

from *Corduroy & Company:
A Don Freeman Treasury*
written and illustrated by Don Freeman

In the beautiful city of San Francisco, a city famous for its fogs and flowers, cable cars and towers, there once stood an electric-light sign on top of a tall building, and inside the letter B of this sign there lived a pigeon.

Before choosing to make his home here this proud gray pigeon had tried living in many other letters in the alphabet. Just why he liked the lower loop of the letter B, no one yet knew.

During the day the wide side walls kept the wind away, and at night the bright lights kept him warm and cozy.

The pigeons who roosted along the ledges of the building across the street thought he was a pretty persnickety pigeon to live where he did. "He's too choosy! He's too choosy!" they would coo.

The only one who never made fun of him was a white-feathered dove. She felt sure he must have a good reason for wanting to live in that letter. Every morning as soon as the sun came up, these two met in mid-air and together they swerved and swooped down into Union Square Park, where they pecked up their breakfast. Mr. Hi Lee was certain to be there, throwing out crumbs from his large paper sack. He would always greet them by saying, "Good morning, Sid and Midge. How are my two early birds?"

All the birds in the city regarded Mr. Hi Lee as their best friend, and he had nicknames for many of them. Sometimes he brought them hard breadcrumbs and sometimes, as an extra-special treat, day-old cake crumbs from a nearby bakery.

After every crumb was pecked up, the pigeons always circled around Mr. Hi Lee's head, flapping their wings as they flew—which was their way of saying, "Thank you!"

By noontime Sid and Midge could be seen sailing high in the sky, flying into one cloud and out the other. Side by side they glided over the bay, until they could look down and see the Golden Gate Bridge.

Sid would swoop and fly through the open arches just to show Midge what a good looper he was.

Then, as the setting sun began painting the sky with a rosy glow, two tuckered out birds would be slowly winging their way back to the pack just in time for supper.

One evening after an especially gay lark in the sky, Sid invited Midge to stay and share his letter B with him.

Across the way pigeons were soon bobbing their heads up and down and cooing, "Whoever heard of birds building a nest in a sign? It'll never do! It'll never do!"

But Sid and Midge went right on building their nest as best they could. They used patches of cloth and strands of string and bits of straw, and gradually there grew a strong nest with a perfect view.

Then one misty morning a few weeks later, just as everything was going along smoothly, something happened which was very upsetting! It occurred right after Sid had flown down to the park to peck up his breakfast. As usual he had left Midge taking her turn sitting on the nest, where there were now two eggs to be kept warm!

Suddenly, like a bolt out of the blue, Midge felt their perch give a terrible lurch! The buildings across the way seemed to sway back and forth. "It's an earthquake!" screeched Midge.

But no—it was even worse than an earthquake! Their sign was being taken down! One by one the letters were being lowered into a waiting truck below. Midge followed, flapping her wings wildly at the movers, trying to let them know they must not take away her nest! But the men paid no attention to her, until the tallest man stopped and shouted, "Hold everything! Look here what I've found! Two eggs in a nest! No wonder that pigeon has been making such a fuss!"

"Well, what do you know!" exclaimed another man as he took a peek inside. "We'll sure have to take good care of this letter. Come to think of it, I know of a bakery shop that could use a big letter 'B.' Anyway, we won't be throwing this one away. Come on, men, let's get going!"

68

Down the hill they went, and far out of sight, with Midge clinging on with all her might!

You can imagine how Sid felt when he landed back on the cold and empty scaffold later that morning! He stood there dazed and bewildered, wondering where his sign had gone. Where was his Midge? And where, oh where, was their nest with those two precious eggs?

He looked around on all sides, but not a trace of his sign did he see. Suddenly off he flew.

First to the waterfront. Possibly the sign was being loaded onto a boat. Sid was sure that wherever that particular letter 'B' was, there, too, Midge would be. He looked high and he looked low, but not a sign of his letter did he spy.

Next he flew to the uppermost post of the Golden Gate Bridge. He thought perhaps Midge might have passed by that way. But no, not a feather did he find.

While he stood wondering where to search next, an enormous fog bank came rolling in from off the ocean. Like a rampaging flock of sheep, the fog came surging straight toward him!

When Sid saw this he puffed out his chest and stretched his wings wide and cried, "Who's afraid of a little breeze? I'll flap my wings and blow the wind away!"

But the fog rolled silently on, and before Sid knew what had happened he was completely surrounded by a dense, damp grayness. And the faster he flew, the thicker the fog grew, until he could barely see beyond his beak. Down, down he dived, hoping to land on solid ground.

All at once he found himself
standing on top of a traffic-light
signal right in the busiest part
of town!

Once inside the green "Go"
signal, Sid began fluffing up his
wings, trying to dry them off before
going on with his search for Midge.

What Sid didn't know was that his
fluffed-up wings hid the word "Go,"
and no one in the street dared to budge.
Soon there was a roar of automobile horns!
"People certainly get awfully upset over a little
fog!" said Sid as he stuck out his head.

Just then along came a policeman, and when he
blew his whistle—BEEEP! BEEEP!—Sid flew out
like a streak of lightning! At last the traffic could
move on!

By now the fog had changed to rain and everybody started hopping aboard the cable cars—which is what people do in San Francisco wherever the hills are too steep or the weather is too wet.

And that's exactly what Sid did! Under the big bell on top of the cable car he found a perfect umbrella.

If only the conductor hadn't shouted, "Hold on tight! Sharp corner ahead!" and then clanged the bell! The clapper of the bell hit Sid so hard that he fell overboard.

In the street gutter below, all bruised and weary, he hobbled along, muttering to himself, "People! It's all people's fault!"

But then he began to think of the kind man in the park. Would Mr. Hi Lee be there on such a terrible day as this? Sid tried to spread his wings and fly, but he was too weak. He would have to walk all the way to Union Square.

Fortunately the park was only a couple of blocks away, and just as Sid hopped up onto the curb he felt a gentle hand reach down and pick him up.

The next thing Sid knew he was inside Mr. Hi Lee's warm overcoat pocket, where, much to his surprise, he found several sunflower seeds. Right away he began to feel better. He could hardly wait to get on with his search for Midge.

When he peeped out, he saw that the rain
had stopped and warm rays from the sun were
beginning to shine down. Mr. Hi Lee talked to
his friend inside his pocket as he walked along.
"Around the corner from here I know of a bakery
where we can get something more for you to eat,"
he said.

As they neared the shop Mr. Hi Lee noticed
some men putting a large letter in the sign above
the doorway. "Well, look at that—a new letter B!"

Out popped Sid's head, farther. What was that
he heard? It sounded exactly like a certain bird
he knew cooing. Could it be?

Yes indeed! It was his very own Midge! She had
stayed with their nest through thick and thin.

Up flew Sid like an arrow shot from a bow. And oh, what a meeting! Such billing and cooing as you've never heard! And no wonder, for their two eggs were just about to hatch!

Out came two tiny beaks breaking through their shells!

And out of the bakery shop came the baker and his customers. They all wanted to know what the excitement was about.

Sid knew that his first duty was to find some food for Midge, so down he flew, and there was Mr. Hi Lee already holding out his hand full of cake crumbs!

After taking the crumbs to Midge, Sid hurried right back down, and this time he circled around and around Mr. Hi Lee's head flapping his wings happily. And we know what he meant by that!

Some time later, when their old neighbors came flying by, they saw Sid and Midge peacefully perched in the lower loop of the letter B and the two little ones in the upper loop. "Oh those lucky birds!" they cooed as they flew away. "Sid certainly did know what he was doing when he chose that letter B!"

About the Author and Illustrator

Don Freeman began his artistic career as a Broadway theater-page illustrator. He eventually left that business and moved to California where he began writing children's picture books. His first book, *Chuggy and the Blue Caboose*, was written for his young son. The inspiration for *Fly High Fly Low* was his favorite city, San Francisco. His most famous work is *Corduroy*. It is one of the earliest picture books to feature African American main characters.

Imagination

The Possible's slow fuse is lit
By the Imagination.
—Emily Dickinson—

Most Beds

from *The Bed Book*

by Sylvia Plath
illustrated by
Emily Arnold McCully

Most Beds are Beds
For sleeping or resting,
But the *best* Beds are much
More interesting!

Not just a white little
Tucked-in-tight little
Nighty-night little
Turn-out-the-light little
　　Bed—

　　Instead
A Bed for Fishing,
A Bed for Cats,
A Bed for a Troupe of
　　Acrobats.

The *right* sort of Bed
(If you see what I mean)
Is a Bed that might
Be a Submarine

Nosing through water
Clear and green,
Silver and glittery
As a sardine

Or a Jet-Propelled Bed
For visiting Mars
With mosquito nets
For the shooting stars . . .

About the Author

One of the most respected poets of the 20th century, **Sylvia Plath** was born in 1932 and had one of her poems published when she was only eight years old. Although Plath wrote primarily for adults, she wrote *The Bed Book* for her two children, Nicholas and Frieda.

Plath's *Collected Poems* won the Pulitzer Prize, an award for exceptional writing. Her most famous works include two other books of poetry entitled *Ariel* and *The Colossus and Other Poems* and an autobiographical novel—*The Bell Jar.*

Margery Williams's daughter Pamela once said that her mother treated the toys in their house as if they were real. In The Velveteen Rabbit, *Williams gives us the story of a stuffed rabbit who becomes "real" because of the love of his owner, the Boy.*

The Velveteen Rabbit

from **The Velveteen Rabbit**

by Margery Williams
illustrated by Jan Palmer

Weeks passed, and the little Rabbit grew very old and shabby, but the Boy loved him just as much. He loved him so hard that he loved all his whiskers off, and the pink lining to his ears turned grey, and his brown spots faded. He even began to lose his shape, and he scarcely looked like a rabbit any more, except to the Boy. To him he was always beautiful, and that was all that the little Rabbit cared about. He didn't mind how he looked to other people, because the nursery magic had made him Real, and when you are Real shabbiness doesn't matter.

And then, one day, the Boy was ill.

His face grew very flushed, and he talked in his sleep, and his little body was so hot that it burned the Rabbit when he held him close. Strange people came and went in the nursery, and a light burned all night and through it all the little Velveteen Rabbit lay there, hidden from sight under the bedclothes, and he never stirred, for he was afraid that if they found him some one might take him away, and he knew that the Boy needed him.

It was a long weary time, for the Boy was too ill to play, and the little Rabbit found it rather dull with nothing to do all day long. But he snuggled down patiently, and looked forward to the time when the Boy should be well again, and they would go out in the garden amongst the flowers and the butterflies and play splendid games in the raspberry thicket like they used to. All sorts of delightful things he planned, and while the Boy lay half asleep he crept up close to the pillow and whispered them in his ear.

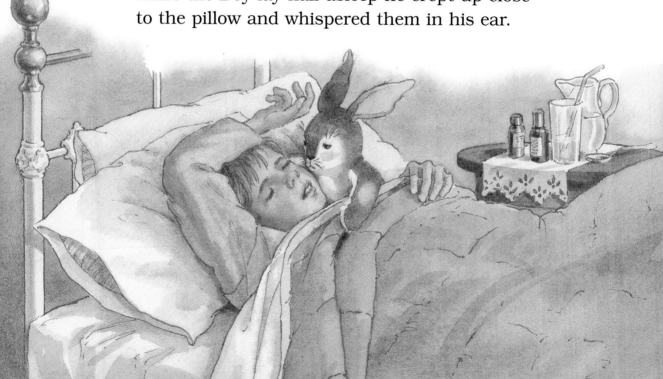

And presently the fever turned, and the Boy got better. He was able to sit up in bed and look at picture books, while the little Rabbit cuddled close at his side. And one day, they let him get up and dress.

It was a bright, sunny morning, and the windows stood wide open. They had carried the Boy out on to the balcony, wrapped in a shawl, and the little Rabbit lay tangled up among the bedclothes, thinking.

The Boy was going to the seaside to-morrow. Everything was arranged, and now it only remained to carry out the doctor's orders. They talked about it all, while the little Rabbit lay under the bedclothes, with just his head peeping out, and listened. The room was to be disinfected, and all the books and toys that the Boy had played with in bed must be burnt.

"Hurrah!" thought the little Rabbit. "To-morrow we shall go to the seaside!" For the Boy had often talked of the seaside, and he wanted very much to see the big waves coming in, and the tiny crabs, and the sand castles.

Just then Nana caught sight of him.

"How about his old Bunny?" she asked.

"*That?*" said the doctor. "Why, it's a mass of scarlet fever germs!—Burn it at once. What? Nonsense! Get him a new one. He mustn't have that any more!"

And so the little Rabbit was put into a sack with the old picture-books and a lot of rubbish, and carried out to the end of the garden behind the fowl-house. That was a fine place to make a bonfire, only the gardener was too busy just then to attend to it. He had the potatoes to dig and the green peas to gather, but next morning he promised to come quite early and burn the whole lot.

That night the Boy slept in a different bedroom, and he had a new bunny to sleep with him. It was a splendid bunny, all white plush with real glass eyes, but the Boy was too excited to care very much about it. For to-morrow he was going to the seaside, and that in itself was such a wonderful thing that he could think of nothing else.

And while the Boy was asleep, dreaming of
the seaside, the little Rabbit lay among the old
picture-books in the corner behind the fowl-house,
and he felt very lonely. The sack had been left
untied, and so by wriggling a bit he was able
to get his head through the opening and look
out. He was shivering a little, for he had always
been used to sleeping in a proper bed, and by
this time his coat had worn so thin and
threadbare from hugging that it was no longer
any protection to him. Near by he could see the
thicket of raspberry canes, growing tall and
close like a tropical jungle, in whose shadow
he had played with the Boy on bygone mornings.

He thought of those long sunlit hours in the
garden—how happy they were—and a great
sadness came over him. He seemed to see them
all pass before him, each more beautiful than
the other, the fairy huts in the flower-bed, the
quiet evenings in the wood when he lay in the
bracken and the little ants ran over his paws;
the wonderful day when he first knew that he
was Real. He thought of the Skin Horse,
so wise and gentle, and all that he had
told him. Of what use was it to be
loved and lose one's beauty and
become Real if it all ended like
this? And a tear, a real tear,
trickled down his little
shabby velvet nose and
fell to the ground.

And then a strange thing happened. For where the tear had fallen a flower grew out of the ground, a mysterious flower, not at all like any that grew in the garden. It had slender green leaves the colour of emeralds, and in the centre of the leaves a blossom like a golden cup. It was so beautiful that the little Rabbit forgot to cry, and just lay there watching it. And presently the blossom opened, and out of it there stepped a fairy.

She was quite the loveliest fairy in the whole world. Her dress was of pearl and dew-drops, and there were flowers round her neck and in her hair, and her face was like the most perfect flower of all. And she came close to the little Rabbit and gathered him up in her arms and kissed him on his velveteen nose that was all damp from crying.

"Little Rabbit," she said, "don't you know who I am?"

The Rabbit looked up at her, and it seemed to him that he had seen her face before, but he couldn't think where.

"I am the nursery magic Fairy," she said. "I take care of all the playthings that the children have loved. When they are old and worn out and the children don't need them any more, then I come take them away with me and turn them into Real."

"Wasn't I Real before?" asked the little Rabbit.

"You were Real to the Boy," the Fairy said, "because he loved you. Now you shall be Real to every one."

And she held the little Rabbit close in her arms and flew with him into the wood.

It was light now, for the moon had risen. All
the forest was beautiful, and the fronds of the
bracken shone like frosted silver. In the open
glade between the tree-trunks the wild rabbits
danced with their shadows on the velvet grass,
but when they saw the Fairy they all stopped
dancing and stood round in a ring to stare at her.

"I've brought you a new playfellow," the Fairy
said. "You must be very kind to him and teach
him all he needs to know in Rabbitland, for he
is going to live with you for ever and ever!"

And she kissed the little Rabbit again and put
him down on the grass.

"Run and play, little Rabbit!" she said.

But the little Rabbit sat quite still for a
moment and never moved. For when he saw
all the wild rabbits dancing around him he
suddenly remembered about his hind legs,
and he didn't want them to see that he was
made all in one piece. He did not know that
when the Fairy kissed him that last time she
had changed him altogether. And he might
have sat there a long time, too shy to move,
if just then something hadn't tickled his nose,
and before he thought what he was doing he
lifted his hind toe to scratch it.

And he found that he actually had hind legs!
Instead of dingy velveteen he had brown fur, soft
and shiny, his ears twitched by themselves, and
his whiskers were so long that they brushed the
grass. He gave one leap and the joy of using those
hind legs was so great that he went springing
about the turf on them, jumping sideways and
whirling round as the others did, and he grew so
excited that when at last he did stop to look for
the Fairy she had gone.

He was a Real Rabbit at last,
at home with the other rabbits.

Autumn passed and Winter, and in the Spring, when the days grew warm and sunny, the Boy went out to play in the wood behind the house. And while he was playing, two rabbits crept out from the bracken and peeped at him. One of them was brown all over, but the other had strange markings under his fur, as though long ago he had been spotted, and the spots still showed through. And about his little soft nose and his round black eyes there was something familiar, so that the Boy thought to himself:

"Why, he looks just like my old Bunny that was lost when I had scarlet fever!"

But he never knew that it really was his own Bunny, come back to look at the child who had first helped him to be Real.

About the Author

Margery Williams was born in London, England, in 1881. She published her first novel when she was only seventeen years old. Her most famous work, *The Velveteen Rabbit,* was the first book she wrote for children. "By thinking about toys and remembering toys, they suddenly became very much alive," said Williams about *The Velveteen Rabbit.*

Many Moons

James Thurber
illustrated by Louis Slobodkin

O nce upon a time, in a kingdom by the sea, there lived a little Princess named Lenore. She was ten years old, going on eleven. One day Lenore fell ill of a surfeit of raspberry tarts and took to her bed.

The Royal Physician came to see her and took her temperature and felt her pulse and made her stick out her tongue. The Royal Physician was worried. He sent for the King, Lenore's father, and the King came to see her.

"I will get you anything your heart desires," the King said. "Is there anything your heart desires?"

"Yes," said the Princess. "I want the moon. If I can have the moon, I will be well again."

Now the King had a great many wise men who always got for him anything he wanted, so he told his daughter that she could have the moon. Then he went to the throne room and pulled a bell cord, three long pulls and a short pull, and presently the Lord High Chamberlain came into the room.

The Lord High Chamberlain was a large, fat man who wore thick glasses which made his eyes seem twice as big as they really were. This made the Lord High Chamberlain seem twice as wise as he really was.

"I want you to get the moon," said the King. "The Princess Lenore wants the moon. If she can have the moon, she will get well again."

"The moon?" exclaimed the Lord High Chamberlain, his eyes widening. This made him look four times as wise as he really was.

"Yes, the moon," said the King. "M-o-o-n, moon. Get it tonight, tomorrow at the latest."

The Lord High Chamberlain wiped his forehead with a handkerchief and then blew his nose loudly. "I have got a great many things for you in my time, your Majesty," he said. "It just happens that I have with me a list of the things I have got for you in my time." He pulled a long scroll of parchment out of his pocket. "Let me see, now."

He glanced at the list, frowning. "I have got ivory, apes, and peacocks, rubies, opals, and emeralds, black orchids, pink elephants, and blue poodles, gold bugs, scarabs, and flies in amber, hummingbirds' tongues, angels' feathers, and unicorns' horns, giants, midgets, and mermaids, frankincense, ambergris, and myrrh, troubadors, minstrels, and dancing women, a pound of butter, two dozen eggs, and a sack of sugar—sorry, my wife wrote that in there."

"I don't remember any blue poodles," said the King.

"It says blue poodles right here on the list, and they are checked off with a little check mark," said the Lord High Chamberlain. "So there must have been blue poodles. You just forget."

"Never mind the blue poodles," said the King. "What I want now is the moon."

"I have sent as far as Samarkand and Araby and Zanzibar to get things for you, your Majesty," said the Lord High Chamberlain. "But the moon is out of the question. It is 35,000 miles away and it is bigger than the room the Princess lies in. Furthermore, it is made of molten copper. I cannot get the moon for you. Blue poodles, yes; the moon, no."

The King flew into a rage and told the Lord High Chamberlain to leave the room and to send the Royal Wizard to the throne room.

The Royal Wizard was a little, thin man with a long face. He wore a high red peaked hat covered with silver stars, and a long blue robe covered with golden owls. His face grew very pale when the King told him he wanted the moon for his little daughter, and that he expected the Royal Wizard to get it.

"I have worked a great deal of magic for you in my time, your Majesty," said the Royal Wizard. "As a matter of fact, I just happen to have in my pocket a list of the wizardries I have performed for you." He drew a paper from a deep pocket of his robe. "It begins: 'Dear Royal Wizard: I am returning herewith the so-called philosopher's stone which you claimed—' no, that isn't it." The Royal Wizard brought a long scroll of parchment from another pocket of his robe.

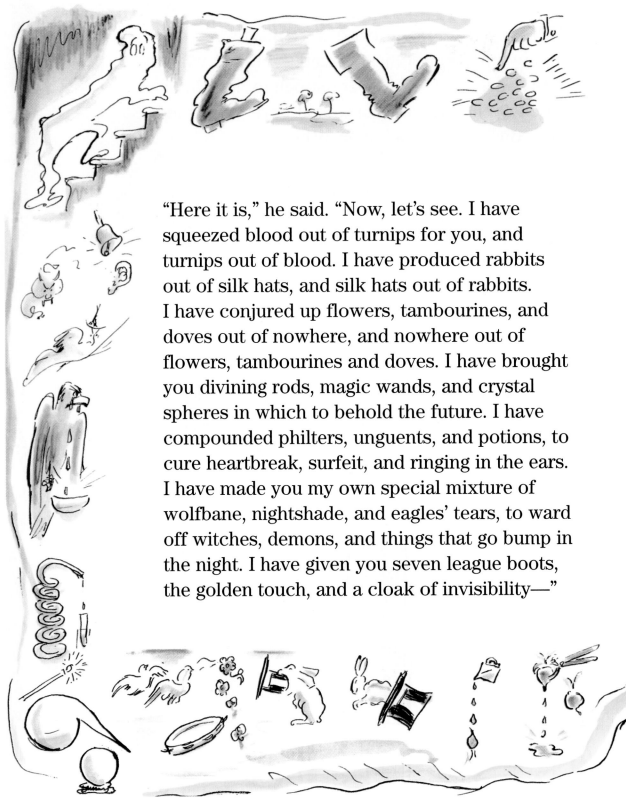

"Here it is," he said. "Now, let's see. I have squeezed blood out of turnips for you, and turnips out of blood. I have produced rabbits out of silk hats, and silk hats out of rabbits. I have conjured up flowers, tambourines, and doves out of nowhere, and nowhere out of flowers, tambourines and doves. I have brought you divining rods, magic wands, and crystal spheres in which to behold the future. I have compounded philters, unguents, and potions, to cure heartbreak, surfeit, and ringing in the ears. I have made you my own special mixture of wolfbane, nightshade, and eagles' tears, to ward off witches, demons, and things that go bump in the night. I have given you seven league boots, the golden touch, and a cloak of invisibility—"

"It didn't work," said the King. "The cloak of invisibility didn't work."

"Yes, it did," said the Royal Wizard.

"No, it didn't," said the King. "I kept bumping into things, the same as ever."

"The cloak is supposed to make you invisible," said the Royal Wizard. "It is not supposed to keep you from bumping into things."

"All I know is, I kept bumping into things," said the King.

The Royal Wizard looked at his list again. "I got you," he said, "horns from Elfland, sand from the Sandman, and gold from the rainbow. Also a spool of thread, a paper of needles, and a lump of beeswax—sorry, those are things my wife wrote down for me to get her."

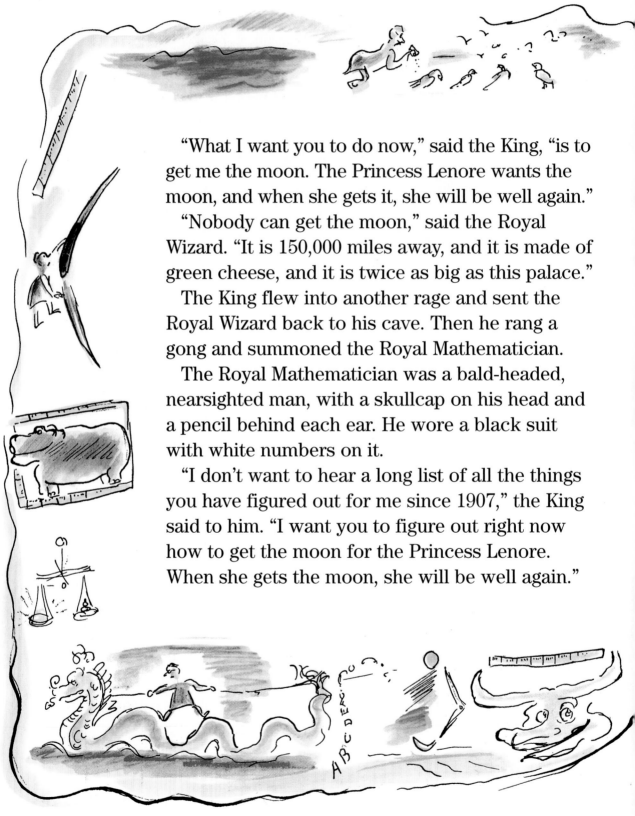

"What I want you to do now," said the King, "is to get me the moon. The Princess Lenore wants the moon, and when she gets it, she will be well again."

"Nobody can get the moon," said the Royal Wizard. "It is 150,000 miles away, and it is made of green cheese, and it is twice as big as this palace."

The King flew into another rage and sent the Royal Wizard back to his cave. Then he rang a gong and summoned the Royal Mathematician.

The Royal Mathematician was a bald-headed, nearsighted man, with a skullcap on his head and a pencil behind each ear. He wore a black suit with white numbers on it.

"I don't want to hear a long list of all the things you have figured out for me since 1907," the King said to him. "I want you to figure out right now how to get the moon for the Princess Lenore. When she gets the moon, she will be well again."

"I am glad you mentioned all the things I have figured out for you since 1907," said the Royal Mathematician. "It so happens that I have a list of them with me."

He pulled a long scroll of parchment out of a pocket and looked at it. "Now let me see. I have figured out for you the distance between the horns of a dilemma, night and day, and A and Z. I have computed how far is Up, how long it takes to get to Away, and what becomes of Gone. I have discovered the length of the sea serpent, the price of the priceless, and the square of the hippopotamus. I know where you are when you are at Sixes and Sevens, how much Is you have to have to make an Are, and how many birds you can catch with the salt in the ocean—187,796,132, if it would interest you to know."

"There aren't that many birds," said the King.

"I didn't say there were," said the Royal Mathematician. "I said if there were."

"I don't want to hear about seven hundred million imaginary birds," said the King. "I want you to get the moon for the Princess Lenore."

"The moon is 300,000 miles away," said the Royal Mathematician. "It is round and flat like a coin, only it is made of asbestos, and it is half the size of this kingdom. Furthermore, it is pasted on the sky. Nobody can get the moon."

The King flew into still another rage and sent the Royal Mathematician away. Then he rang for the Court Jester. The Jester came bounding into the throne room in his motley and his cap and bells, and sat at the foot of the throne.

"What can I do for you, your Majesty?" asked the Court Jester.

"Nobody can do anything for me," said the King mournfully. "The Princess Lenore wants the moon, and she cannot be well till she gets it, but nobody can get it for her. Every time I ask anybody for the moon, it gets larger and farther away. There is nothing you can do for me except play on your lute. Something sad."

"How big do they say the moon is," asked the Court Jester, "and how far away?"

"The Lord High Chamberlain says it is 35,000 miles away, and bigger than the Princess Lenore's room," said the King. "The Royal Wizard says it is 150,000 miles away, and twice as big as this palace. The Royal Mathematician says it is 300,000 miles away, and half the size of this kingdom."

The Court Jester strummed on his lute for a little while. "They are all wise men," he said, "and so they must all be right. If they are all right, then the moon must be just as large and as far away as each person thinks it is. The thing to do is find out how big the Princess Lenore thinks it is, and how far away."

"I never thought of that," said the King.

"I will go and ask her, your Majesty," said the Court Jester. And he crept softly into the little girl's room.

The Princess Lenore was awake, and she was glad to see the Court Jester, but her face was very pale and her voice very weak.

"Have you brought the moon to me?" she asked.

"Not yet," said the Court Jester, "but I will get it for you right away. How big do you think it is?"

"It is just a little smaller than my thumbnail," she said, "for when I hold my thumbnail up at the moon, it just covers it."

"And how far away is it?" asked the Court Jester.

"It is not as high as the big tree outside my window," said the Princess, "for sometimes it gets caught in the top branches."

"It will be very easy to get the moon for you," said the Court Jester. "I will climb the tree tonight when it gets caught in the top branches and bring it to you."

Then he thought of something else. "What is the moon made of, Princess?" he asked.

"Oh," she said, "it's made of gold, of course, silly."

The Court Jester left the Princess Lenore's room and went to see the Royal Goldsmith. He had the Royal Goldsmith make a tiny round golden moon just a little smaller than the thumbnail of the Princess Lenore. Then he had him string it on a golden chain so the Princess could wear it around her neck.

"What is this thing I have made?" asked the Royal Goldsmith when he had finished it.

"You have made the moon," said the Court Jester. "That is the moon."

"But the moon," said the Royal Goldsmith, "is 500,000 miles away and is made of bronze and is round like a marble."

"That's what you think," said the Court Jester as he went away with the moon.

The Court Jester took the moon to the Princess Lenore, and she was overjoyed. The next day she was well again and could get up and go out in the gardens to play.

But the King's worries were not yet over. He knew that the moon would shine in the sky again that night, and he did not want the Princess Lenore to see it. If she did, she would know that the moon she wore on a chain around her neck was not the real moon.

So the King sent for the Lord High Chamberlain and said, "We must keep the Princess Lenore from seeing the moon when it shines in the sky tonight. Think of something."

The Lord High Chamberlain tapped his forehead with his fingers thoughtfully and said, "I know just the thing. We can make some dark glasses for the Princess Lenore. We can make them so dark that she will not be able to see anything at all through them. Then she will not be able to see the moon when it shines in the sky."

This made the King very angry, and he shook his head from side to side. "If she wore dark glasses, she would bump into things," he said, "and then she would be ill again." So he sent the Lord High Chamberlain away and called the Royal Wizard.

"We must hide the moon," said the King, "so that the Princess Lenore will not see it when it shines in the sky tonight. How are we going to do that?"

The Royal Wizard stood on his hands and then he stood on his head and then he stood on his feet again. "I know what we can do," he said. "We can stretch some black velvet curtains on poles. The curtains will cover all the palace gardens like a circus tent, and the Princess Lenore will not be able to see through them, so she will not see the moon in the sky."

The King was so angry at this that he waved his arms around. "Black velvet curtains would keep out the air," he said. "The Princess Lenore would not be able to breathe, and she would be ill again." So he sent the Royal Wizard away and summoned the Royal Mathematician.

"We must do something," said the King, "so that Princess Lenore will not see the moon when it shines in the sky tonight. If you know so much, figure out a way to do that."

The Royal Mathematician walked around in a circle, and then he walked around in a square, and then he stood still. "I have it!" he said. "We can set off fireworks in the gardens every night. We will make a lot of silver fountains and golden cascades, and when they go off, they will fill the sky with so many sparks that it will be as light as day and the Princess Lenore will not be able to see the moon."

The King flew into such a rage that he began jumping up and down. "Fireworks would keep the Princess Lenore awake," he said. "She would not get any sleep at all and she would be ill again." So the King sent the Royal Mathematician away.

When he looked up again, it was dark outside and he saw the bright rim of the moon just peeping over the horizon. He jumped up in a great fright and rang for the Court Jester. The Court Jester came bounding into the room and sat down at the foot of the throne.

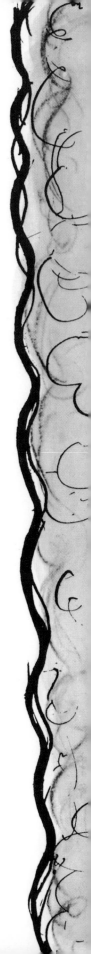

"What can I do for you, your Majesty?" he asked.

"Nobody can do anything for me," said the King, mournfully. "The moon is coming up again. It will shine into Princess Lenore's bedroom, and she will know it is still in the sky and that she does not wear it on a golden chain around her neck. Play me something on your lute, something very sad, for when the Princess sees the moon, she will be ill again."

The Court Jester strummed on his lute. "What do your wise men say?" he asked.

"They can think of no way to hide the moon that will not make the Princess Lenore ill," said the King.

The Court Jester played another song, very softly. "Your wise men know everything," he said, "and if they cannot hide the moon, then it cannot be hidden."

The King put his head in his hands again and sighed. Suddenly he jumped up from his throne and pointed to the windows. "Look!" he cried. "The moon is already shining into the Princess Lenore's bedroom. Who can explain how the moon can be shining in the sky when it is hanging on a golden chain around her neck?"

The Court Jester stopped playing on his lute. "Who could explain how to get the moon when your wise men said it was too large and too far away? It was the Princess Lenore. Therefore the Princess Lenore is wiser than your wise men and knows more about the moon than they do. So I will ask *her*." And before the King could stop him, the Court Jester slipped quietly out of the throne room and up the wide marble staircase to the Princess Lenore's bedroom.

The Princess was lying in bed, but she was wide awake and she was looking out the window at the moon shining in the sky. Shining in her hand was the moon the Court Jester had got for her. He looked very sad, and there seemed to be tears in his eyes.

"Tell me, Princess Lenore," he said mournfully, "how can the moon be shining in the sky when it is hanging on a golden chain around your neck?"

The Princess looked at him and laughed. "That is easy, silly," she said. "When I lose a tooth, a new one grows in its place, doesn't it?"

"Of course," said the Court Jester. "And when the unicorn loses his horn in the forest, a new one grows in the middle of his forehead."

"That is right," said the Princess. "And when the Royal Gardener cuts the flowers in the garden, other flowers come to take their place."

"I should have thought of that," said the Court Jester, "for it is the same way with the daylight."

"And it is the same way with the moon," said the Princess Lenore. "I guess it is the same way with everything." Her voice became very low and faded away, and the Court Jester saw that she was asleep. Gently he tucked the covers in around the sleeping Princess.

But before he left the room, he went over to the window and winked at the moon, for it seemed to the Court Jester that the moon had winked at him.

About the Author

James Thurber was born in Columbus, Ohio, in 1894. From an early age, he showed an interest in writing and drawing. These talents would serve him for the rest of his life.

Thurber is considered to be one of the most important figures in American humor. He is best remembered as a writer and cartoonist for *The New Yorker* and as the author of the short stories "The Secret Life of Walter Mitty" and "The Catbird Seat." *Many Moons* is one of the five children's books Thurber wrote.

UNIT

4

Money

To learn the value of money, it is not
necessary to know the nice things
it can get for you, you have to have
experienced the trouble of getting it.
—Philippe Hériat—

A Chair for My Mother

written and illustrated by Vera B. Williams

My mother works as a waitress in the Blue Tile Diner. After school sometimes I go to meet her there. Then her boss Josephine gives me a job too.

I wash the salts and peppers and fill the ketchups. One time I peeled all the onions for the onion soup. When I finish, Josephine says, "Good work, honey," and pays me. And every time, I put half of my money into the jar.

It takes a long time to fill a jar this big. Every day when my mother comes home from work, I take down the jar. My mama empties all her change from tips out of her purse for me to count. Then we push all of the coins into the jar.

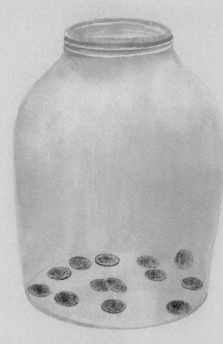

Sometimes my mama is laughing when she comes home from work. Sometimes she's so tired she falls asleep while I count the money out into piles. Some days she has lots of tips. Some days she has only a little. Then she looks worried. But each evening every single shiny coin goes into the jar.

We sit in the kitchen to count the tips. Usually Grandma sits with us too. While we count, she likes to hum. Often she has money in her old leather wallet for us. Whenever she gets a good bargain on tomatoes or bananas or something she buys, she puts by the savings and they go into the jar.

When we can't get a single other coin into the jar, we are going to take out all the money and go and buy a chair.

Yes, a chair. A wonderful, beautiful, fat, soft armchair. We will get one covered in velvet with roses all over it. We are going to get the best chair in the whole world.

That is because our old chairs burned up. There was a big fire in our other house. All our chairs burned. So did our sofa and so did everything else. That wasn't such a long time ago.

My mother and I were coming home from buying new shoes. I had new sandals. She had new pumps. We were walking to our house from the bus. We were looking at everyone's tulips. She was saying she liked red tulips and I was saying I liked yellow ones. Then we came to our block.

Right outside our house stood two big fire
engines. I could see lots of smoke. Tall orange
flames came out of the roof. All the neighbors
stood in a bunch across the street. Mama grabbed
my hand and we ran. My uncle Sandy saw us and
ran to us. Mama yelled, "Where's Mother?" I
yelled, "Where's my grandma?" My aunt Ida waved
and shouted, "She's here, she's here. She's O.K.
Don't worry."

Grandma was all right. Our cat was safe too,
though it took a while to find her. But everything
else in our whole house was spoiled.

What was left of the house was turned to
charcoal and ashes.

We went to stay with my mother's sister Aunt Ida and Uncle Sandy. Then we were able to move into the apartment downstairs. We painted the walls yellow. The floors were all shiny. But the rooms were very empty.

The first day we moved in, the neighbors brought pizza and cake and ice cream. And they brought a lot of other things too.

The family across the street brought a table and three kitchen chairs. The very old man next door gave us a bed from when his children were little.

My other grandpa brought us his beautiful rug.
My mother's other sister, Sally, had made us red
and white curtains. Mama's boss, Josephine,
brought pots and pans, silverware and dishes.
My cousin brought me her own stuffed bear.

Everyone clapped when my grandma made a
speech. "You are all the kindest people," she said,
"and we thank you very, very much. It's lucky
we're young and can start all over."

That was last year, but we still have no sofa and no big chairs. When Mama comes home, her feet hurt. "There's no good place for me to take a load off my feet," she says. When Grandma wants to sit back and hum and cut up potatoes, she has to get as comfortable as she can on a hard kitchen chair.

So that is how come Mama brought home the biggest jar she could find at the diner and all the coins started to go into the jar.

Now the jar is too heavy for me to lift down. Uncle Sandy gave me a quarter. He had to boost me up so I could put it in.

After supper Mama and Grandma and I stood in front of the jar. "Well, I never would have believed it, but I guess it's full," Mama said.

A Chair for My Mother

My mother brought home little paper wrappers
for the nickels and the dimes and the quarters.
I counted them all out and wrapped them all up.

On my mother's day off, we took all the coins
to the bank. The bank exchanged them
for ten-dollar bills. Then we took the
bus downtown to shop for our chair.

We shopped through four furniture stores. We
tried out big chairs and smaller ones, high chairs
and low chairs, soft chairs and harder ones.
Grandma said she felt like Goldilocks in "The
Three Bears" trying out all the chairs.

Finally we found the chair we were all dreaming
of. And the money in the jar was enough to pay for
it. We called Aunt Ida and Uncle Sandy. They came
right down in their pickup truck to drive the chair
home for us. They knew we couldn't wait for it to
be delivered.

I tried out our chair in the back of the truck. Mama wouldn't let me sit there while we drove. But they let me sit in it while they carried it up to the door.

We set the chair right beside the window with the red and white curtains. Grandma and Mama and I all sat in it while Aunt Ida took our picture.

Now Grandma sits in it and talks with people going by in the daytime. Mama sits down and watches the news on TV when she comes home from her job. After supper, I sit with her and she can reach right up and turn out the light if I fall asleep in her lap.

About the Author and Illustrator

Vera B. Williams didn't begin creating children's books until she was in her late forties. However, she had been an artist since childhood. When she was just nine years old, the Museum of Modern Art in New York City exhibited one of her paintings.

A Chair for My Mother, like many of Williams's books, was inspired by events in her life. Williams said the book is "a kind of gift to my mother's memory." The characters from *A Chair for My Mother* appear in two other books, *Something Special for Me* and *Music, Music for Everyone*.

Henry Gets Rich

from *Henry and Beezus*

by Beverly Cleary

illustrated by Brock Nicol

Henry Huggins wants a bicycle. He has only one problem: he doesn't have enough money to buy one. His latest plan to earn money is to sell the boxes of bubble gum he recently found. His friend, Beezus, decides to help him. However, Henry soon discovers that selling something for profit is no easy matter.

As soon as he reached Glenwood School, boys and girls began to crowd around him. "Did you get to keep all that gum Mary Jane said you found in the lot?" they asked.

"Sure I got to keep it," said Henry, disappointed at having his surprise spoiled. If that wasn't just like a girl, especially Mary Jane. "I'm going to sell it two for a penny."

The boys and girls knew a bargain when they saw one. "I'll take four," said Joey.

"Give me two," said Peter.

Some of the children did not have money with them, but Henry said they could bring it the next day. He opened charge accounts by writing their names and the amounts they owed on the margin of a comic book he had in the hip pocket of his jeans. By the time the second bell rang, Henry had twenty-two cents coming to him. Boy, oh, boy, he thought. This is even better than I expected.

By noon the news of Henry's treasure had spread throughout the school, and boys and girls from other rooms crowded around to buy the bargain gum. Henry was so busy selling that Beezus offered to write down the names of those who were going to bring their money the next day. By the time school was out, Henry had fifty-one cents in real money and forty-three cents written in his comic book. That was almost a dollar for his bike fund. Besides that, he had four marbles, a yo-yo, and six comic books.

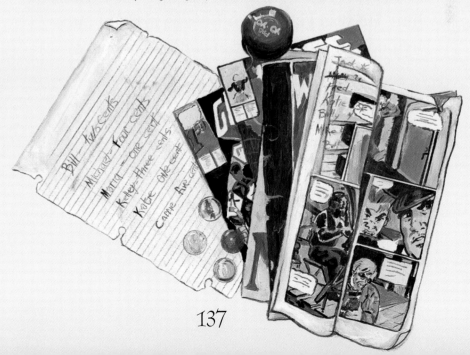

And that was not all. Joey chose him to be the next blackboard monitor, Kathleen said she was going to invite him to her birthday party, six boys wanted to sit beside him in the cafeteria at noon, and Roger rode him home on his bicycle.

The next day Henry left even earlier and took another box of gum to school. He found business more complicated, because he not only had to sell gum and write down the names of the boys and girls who would bring their money the next day, he had to cross off in his comic book the names of those who had remembered to bring the pennies they owed him. He was glad when Beezus arrived and helped him keep the transactions straight.

At first, the boys and girls who were chewing Henry's gum were careful to chew only when Miss Bonner wasn't looking, but after a while they forgot to be careful. Then she said unexpectedly, "Henry, tell the class what mark of punctuation should go at the end of the sentence I have written on the blackboard."

Taken by surprise, Henry quickly shifted his quid of gum to his cheek. "A period . . . uh . . . I mean a question mark," he said.

"I think, Henry," said Miss Bonner, "that if you throw your gum in the wastebasket, we shall all have much less trouble understanding you."

Feeling foolish, Henry walked to the front of the room and threw his wad of gum into the empty metal wastebasket. When it landed with a loud *clonk*, the whole class tittered.

"And now," said Miss Bonner, "I want everyone in the room who has gum in his or her mouth to throw it into the wastebasket."

Sheepishly, half a dozen boys and Beezus walked to the wastebasket and discarded their gum.

Miss Bonner looked around the room. "Robert," she said sternly. "George." The two boys slouched to the wastebasket.

After recess Miss Bonner marched another procession of gum chewers to the wastebasket. Although she didn't say much, Henry decided she looked pretty cross.

When Henry carried his gum out to the playground at noon, he found to his surprise that no one wanted to buy. Nearly everyone was already chewing and blowing.

"Maybe if you cut the price you could sell more," suggested Beezus.

"I guess I'll have to," said Henry. "I'll try four for a penny."

SALE
Four For
a Penny!

141

Business picked up after that, but when Henry went home after school, he wasn't sure how much money he had. He actually had thirty-one cents in his pocket, but when he tried to figure out the accounts in the comic book, he had to give up. Some of the boys who had forgotten to bring their money had charged more gum. Some had paid, but he had forgotten to cross off their names. Anyway, the comic book was getting so ragged and dirty, and the pencil marks so smudged, that it was impossible to read anything. Tossing the book into the fireplace, Henry decided he could remember how much Roger and Peter and a few more owed. He would just have to hope the others paid him.

The next morning when Henry was about to start to school with a box of gum, Beezus rang the doorbell. She handed Henry her box of bubble gum. "Mother says I have to give this back to you," she said.

"What for?" asked Henry.

"Because of Ramona. She gets into the gum and chews it and gets it stuck in her hair. The only way Mother can get it out is to cut it out with the scissors. Ramona looks pretty awful with her hair all different lengths, and Daddy says if this keeps up she'll be bald before long." Beezus looked apologetic. "Anyway, I'm kind of tired of chewing gum."

When they reached the playground, Henry found business slow; everyone was already chewing gum. But when Henry cut the price to ten balls for a penny, he made several sales.

"Do you have any flavors beside cinnamon-peppermint or whatever it is?" asked Joey.

Henry had to admit he did not.

"Oh," said Joey, and went away.

Henry tried to think what stores did when they wanted to sell something. He knew they had sales, they advertised, and they gave away free samples. Henry had tried gum sales and he couldn't think of a good way to advertise, so he decided to try free samples. Although a dozen children crowded around him for samples, the demand was not as large as he had expected.

Then Roger, who owed Henry four cents for gum, approached him and asked for a free sample. Henry wasn't sure whether he should give gum to someone who owed him money, but since he had given it to the others, he gave Roger a piece. Roger put it in his pocket.

"How about that four cents you owe me for eight balls of gum you bought yesterday?" asked Henry.

"I forgot it," said Roger. "And anyway, how come you're giving gum away today when you sold it yesterday?"

"Well . . . " Henry didn't like to admit that no one was interested in his gum.

"Yes," said Peter, joining in the conversation. "I don't see why I have to pay you. You're giving it away now."

"I wasn't giving it away yesterday and the day before," said Henry. "I was selling it, so you owe me money."

"I do not." Peter blew a bubble that popped.

"You do too," said Henry, feeling confused.

The bell rang, and they started toward their classroom. Henry noticed Peter and Roger talking to each other. Then they gathered a bunch of children around them outside the door. They talked earnestly together until Miss Bonner herded them into the room.

Now what are they up to? thought Henry. He worried about it all through social studies and arithmetic. Somehow, things didn't seem to be turning out the way he had planned. He was secretly pleased when Miss Bonner made Peter throw his gum in the wastebasket.

When recess came, Henry was surprised at the number of boys and girls who suddenly wanted free gum. He had almost as big a crowd around him as he had had on the first morning. He began to enjoy himself again.

Then Roger and Peter called to him. "Hey, Henry, can we see you a sec?"

"Sure," said Henry, stepping away from the others.

"Here's the gum I owe you." Roger handed Henry eight balls of bubble gum.

"Mine, too." Peter held out four balls.

"Hey, now wait a minute," protested Henry. "That's not fair."

"It is too," said Roger. "We bought gum from you and now we're returning it instead of paying for it."

"But you chewed it," objected Henry. "I saw you, and Miss Bonner made you throw it in the wastebasket."

"This gum hasn't been chewed, has it?" asked Peter.

Henry had to admit it hadn't.

"Then why can't we return it, like in a department store?" demanded Roger.

Baffled, Henry took the gum. Something was wrong some place, but he couldn't figure out what. He did know one thing, that was sure. There went six cents out of his bike fund.

Then Mary Jane ran up to Roger and Peter. "Did he take the free samples we collected for you?" she asked.

"Well, how do you like that!" exclaimed Henry. "That's cheating, that's what it is."

"It is not," said Mary Jane. "You gave us the gum and if we want to give it to someone else, that's our business."

Henry looked glum. He supposed it was her business. Mary Jane was one of those annoying girls who were always right. The worst of it was, now he couldn't expect the others to pay. Henry was actually glad when the bell ended recess, even though he knew spelling came next.

That day no one chose Henry to be a monitor, and only Robert sat with him in the cafeteria. He heard Kathleen say she thought she wouldn't invite any boys to her birthday party.

About the Author

Beverly Cleary, born in 1916, began writing books with one goal in mind: to capture the lives and adventures of ordinary children. If her popularity is any indication of her success, she has achieved her goal. Cleary has won many awards for her writing. For example, she won a Newbery Medal for *Dear Mr. Henshaw* and a Laura Ingalls Wilder Award for lifetime achievement.

The Silver Penny

Hans Christian Andersen
illustrated by Pat Paris

There was a penny that had come bright from the mint, skipping and clinking. "Hurrah!" it cried. "I'm off into the wide world!" And it was.

The child held on to it tightly with warm hands and the miser with cold and clammy hands; old people turned it over and over many times, while the young sent it rolling on at once. The penny was a silver one with just a little copper in it; and it had been a whole year in the world—that is to say, in the country where it had been minted— when, one day, it went on a journey abroad. It was the last of the country's coins that were left in the purse of its traveling master, and he had no idea that he had it till it got between his fingers.

The Silver Penny

"Why, I've still got a penny from home!" he said. "It can travel along with me." And the penny clinked and skipped for joy as he put it back into the purse. It lay there with foreign companions who came and went; one would make way for the next, but always the penny from home stayed behind. That was a distinction.

Several weeks had now gone by, and the penny was far out in the world, without exactly knowing where; it heard from the other coins that they were French and Italian, and one would say that now they were in this town, and another would say that now they were in that; but of all this the penny could have no idea, for you don't see the world when you're always in a bag, which is where it was.

But noticing one day that the purse wasn't shut, it crept to the opening in order to peep out. Now this it should never have done, but then it was inquisitive, and you have to pay for that: it fell out into the trouser pocket, and when the purse was laid aside in the evening, the penny was left where it was and went with the clothes into the corridor; there it dropped straight onto the floor, and nobody heard it, nobody saw it.

In the morning the clothes were brought in, and the gentleman put them on and went away. And the penny didn't go with him, but was found, put into service again, and went out with three other coins.

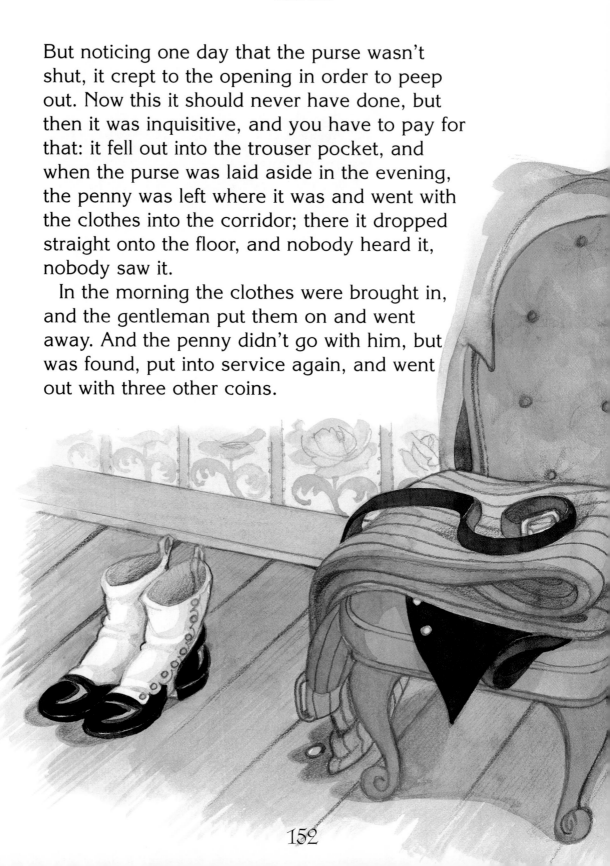

Well, it's nice to see the world! thought the penny. To know other people, other customs!

"What sort of a penny's this?" somebody said all at once. "This isn't our money! It's false! No good!"

And here begins the penny's story, as it afterwards told it.

"False! No good! It cut me," said the penny. "I knew I was of good silver and good ring, and of good mint. Surely they were mistaken and couldn't mean me! But they did mean me! It was me they were calling false! Me that was no good! 'I'll have to pass this in the dark!' said the man who had me. And so I was passed in the dark and abused in broad daylight. "False! No good! We must get rid of this."

And the penny would tremble in the fingers every time it was to be secretly passed off as lawful coin.

"Miserable me!" said the penny, "What was the use of silver, my stamp, my mint, when they didn't mean anything? Your worth to the world is the value the world puts on you. How awful to have a guilty conscience and slink along paths of wickedness when I, though I was perfectly innocent, could feel as I did by only seeming to! Every time I was taken out I dreaded the eyes that would look at me, for I knew that I should be thrust back and flung on the counter, as if I were a cheat and a liar.

"Once I was passed to a poor penniless woman who got me in payment for her daily labor, and she was unable to get rid of me. Nobody would have me; I was a real trouble to her.

"'I can't help it, I shall have to cheat somebody with it,' she said. 'I can't afford to hold on to a bad penny. The rich baker shall have it; he can best afford it. But I shall still be doing wrong.'

"So now I'm going to trouble the woman's conscience!" I sighed. "Can I really have changed so very much in my old age?"

"And so the woman went to the rich baker's; but he knew, only too well, what coins were lawful. I didn't stay long where I was laid, but was flung in the woman's face; she got no bread for me, and I was made thoroughly miserable by having been thus minted for others' misfortune; I who in my younger days had been so cheerful and so confident, so conscious of my value and my goodness.

I grew as melancholy as a poor penny can when nobody will have it. But taking me back home the woman looked at me very gently and with great kindness and friendliness. 'No,' she said, 'I shan't cheat anybody with you! I'll punch a hole in you so everybody can see you're a bad one. And yet, come to think of it, you may be a lucky penny. Yes, I do believe! It's an idea! I'll punch a hole, thread a string through it, and then give the penny to the neighbor's little girl to hang round her neck for luck!'

"And so she punched a hole in me. It's never very nice to have a hole punched in you, but when the intention's good, you can put up with a good deal. I was threaded and so became a sort of medal to be worn. I was hung round the little child's neck; and the child smiled at me and kissed me.

"In the morning her mother took me between her fingers and looked at me, thinking to herself as she did so, as I soon realized. Getting out a pair of scissors she cut the thread.

"'Lucky penny!' she said. 'Well, we'll soon see!' And so saying she put me in acid, and made me turn green; whereupon she sealed up the hole, rubbed me a little, and went off in the dark to the lottery agent for a lottery ticket that would bring good luck.

"How miserable I felt! I was so crushed that I could have snapped in two. I knew I should be called bad and flung back, and, what's more, in the sight of all those pennies and shillings with inscriptions and faces they could be proud of. But I escaped. There were so many people at the agent's, and he was so busy, that I fell clinking into the till with all the other coins.

Whether the ticket ever won a prize I cannot say, but I do know that I was recognized as a bad penny the very next day, put on one side, and sent out to cheat, always cheat. It's unbearable when you're an honest character as I declare I am.

"Year by year I thus passed from hand to hand and from house to house, always being abused and always looked down on; nobody believed in me, and I didn't even believe in myself or in the world. It was a hard time.

"Then one day a traveller came and, of course, I was made to cheat him, and he was innocent enough to take me for good money; but he was just about to spend me when once more I heard the cries of 'No good! False!'

"'I took it for a good one,' said the man, taking a closer look at me. Then all at once his face lit up, as no other face had ever done on giving me a closer look, as he said: 'Why, what's this? If it isn't one of our own coins; a good honest penny from home with a hole punched in it, and they're calling it bad. Well, this is funny! I shall keep you and take you back home with me!'

"I was thrilled with joy: I had been called a good, honest penny and was going back home where everybody would know me and tell that I was of good silver and true coin. I could have sparked for joy, only it isn't my nature to spark: that's for steel to do, not silver.

"I was wrapped up in fine white paper so that I shouldn't get mixed up with the other coins and be lost, and was only taken out on special occasions when fellow countrymen got together, and then was extremely well spoken of. They said I was interesting; and it's a pleasant thought that you can be interesting without saying a word.

"And so I came home! My troubles were all over, and my joys were beginning; for I was of good silver, and I had the right stamp, and it didn't do the slightest harm having a hole punched in me for being bad because it doesn't matter when you aren't. You have to hold out, for everything will come right in the end! Well, that's my belief!" said the penny.

About the Author

What do the stories of the Ugly Duckling, the Little Mermaid, and Thumbelina have in common? **Hans Christian Andersen** wrote all these tales and many more. Born in Denmark in 1805, Andersen didn't let a difficult, often penniless, childhood discourage him. Like the silver penny, he believed you had "to hold out, for everything will come right in the end!" He used his talent as a writer to change his financial situation. He became a famous novelist. Andersen wrote novels, short stories, and travel books. His fairy tales made him a celebrity around the world.

Storytelling

The universe is made of stories, not atoms.
—Muriel Rukeyser—

ARACHNE THE WEAVER

A GREEK MYTH RETOLD

Carol Ottolenghi
illustrated by Nilesh Mistry

Arachne was famous for two things. One was her weaving. The colorful flowers in her cloth looked so real that people stopped to sniff them. And the material felt as soft and light as clouds.

Every day, Arachne set up her loom in a shady corner of the town square. There was always a crowd around her. Women getting water from the well in the square stopped to see what she was weaving. Merchants from all over Greece came to buy her cloth. Nymphs and other magical beings joined the crowd around the girl, too.

One afternoon, a water nymph stopped
to watch.

Woosh, woosh.

Arachne had stretched many shades of blue
thread across her loom. Her right hand threw
her wooden shuttle across the web of threads.
She caught the shuttle with her left hand and
threw it back. Every *woosh* of the shuttle
added another thread to the long cloth she
was weaving.

The water nymph laughed with delight.
She picked up the end of the cloth, and then
let it flow from her hands to the ground.

"You have woven a waterfall!" the water
nymph cried. "It is so beautiful. It reminds me
of my river. Athena, the goddess who inspires
all of the home arts, must have taught you!"

165

Arachne was famous for two things. One was her weaving.

The other thing was her pride.

"Athena did not teach me to weave," Arachne said. She tossed her curly dark hair back and stuck her chin in the air. "How could she teach me? I am a better weaver than she is."

The crowd around her gasped.

An old woman knocked her walking staff against Arachne's loom. "Careful with your words, girl," she said. "It is good to feel joy when you do something well. But don't make foolish boasts because of your pride. You could not weave at all if Athena had not given you the gift. You should ask the goddess to forgive you."

Arachne frowned. She knew
her skill at weaving was a gift from
Athena. But Arachne didn't like to
admit it. She snapped her thread
and stood.

"Mind your own business," she
told the old woman. "I wasn't
helped by Athena or anyone else."

Suddenly the old woman
straightened. She grew tall and
majestic. A shiny helmet crowned
her golden hair. It was Athena.

167

The crowd backed up in alarm. Gods and goddesses often pretended to be humans. But they only showed themselves when they were very pleased or very angry. Everyone knew that Athena wasn't pleased.

"I repeat," she said in a stern voice, "you should ask the goddess to forgive you."

Arachne's face was pale and her lips trembled. But she swallowed hard and said, "I won't. In fact, I challenge you to a contest."

Athena's gray eyes flashed with anger. The goddess struck the dusty ground with her staff. A loom sprang from the earth. The goddess and the girl began to weave.

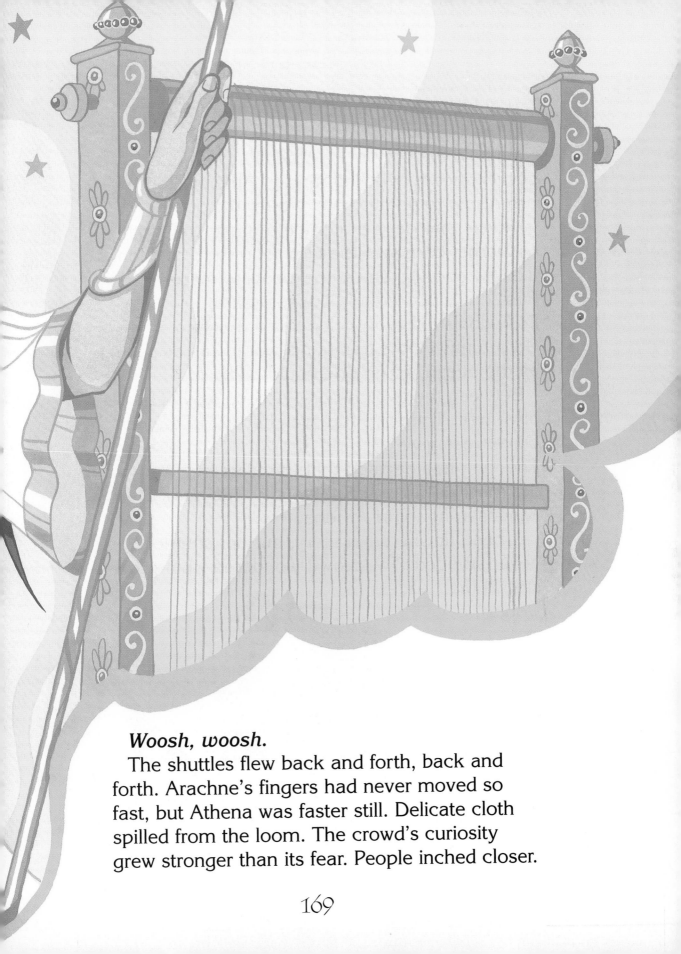

Woosh, woosh.
The shuttles flew back and forth, back and forth. Arachne's fingers had never moved so fast, but Athena was faster still. Delicate cloth spilled from the loom. The crowd's curiosity grew stronger than its fear. People inched closer.

"Look!" cried a merchant. "The goddess weaves the story of Athens."

He held the bottom of Athena's cloth. One corner showed the first king of Athens. He was promising to name the city after the god or goddess that gave the city the most useful gift.

Another corner of the cloth showed Poseidon, the sea god. Athena's fine weaving made Poseidon's beard look like sea foam. Poseidon's gift to the city was a fountain. Unfortunately, the fountain's water was as salty as the ocean, so no one could drink it.

Between the two corners, Athena wove an olive tree. The olive tree was her gift to the city. Olive trees give oil, food, firewood, and beauty. The king had decided that the olive tree was the most useful gift. So, the city was named Athens in honor of Athena.

Athena finished that story, but her shuttle never stopped. The crowd wondered what other stories the goddess would weave.

Athena's fingers moved quickly. She wove a lovely woman. The woman was admiring herself in a mirror and laughing at the goddess. In the next picture, Athena had turned the woman into a crane.

Finally, Athena wove a calm pool of water in the forest. A man kneeled near the pool. He held his hands over his eyes.

The crowd did not know this story right away. Finally, a woman said, "It's Teiresias! He saw Athena by accident, and the goddess blinded him."

Arachne bit her lip. All of Athena's pictures showed the goddess winning contests or punishing humans who angered her. Athena was warning Arachne to admit that her skill was a gift from the goddess.

But Arachne wouldn't admit it. Instead, she wove stories that made fun of Athena.

First, she wove an image of Athena inventing the flute. The goddess played it so sweetly that birds stopped their singing to listen. Then Arachne showed Athena admiring herself in a brass mirror. Athena looked horrified at how red and puffed out her cheeks were, and she threw away her silver pipe.

Arachne laughed aloud as she started weaving the next story. The crowd moved closer to her loom to see what it was.

"It's a wedding banquet," cried a girl. Water sloshed from the water jar on her head as she spoke. "All the gods and goddesses are there."

"See the golden apple?" said a woman. "It must be the wedding of Peleus and Thetis."

"That's right!" replied the girl. "She's weaving the Judgment of Paris."

"And here," a merchant touched the cloth, "the goddesses make their promises to Paris. Hera promises him power and riches. See the crown surrounded by diamonds and rubies?"

"This must be Athena. How gray her eyes are!" said a young woman. "She promises Paris glory in war. Look at the crossed spears and gold helmets lying at her feet."

"There's Aphrodite; how lovely she is!" said a young man about the image. "She offers Paris the most beautiful woman in the world, Helen."

"Here's Paris picking Aphrodite as the prettiest goddess," said an old man. "Hera and Athena look so jealous and angry! Athena's cheeks are crimson red. Just like in the story of the flute."

"Even goddesses can look foolish, and they don't always win," said Arachne with another laugh.

Athena was furious when she heard that. She stood and glared at Arachne's cloth. Every picture was an insult.

But Athena was amazed at the girl's skill. Arachne's birds seemed ready to fly off the material. The light in the diamonds flickered and danced. The colors glowed. There were no mistakes. The story pictures were perfect.

The goddess smiled. It was not a nice smile.

"You win, Arachne," she said. "What shall I give you as a prize? I know. You and your family will be famous weavers forever. But, people will always destroy what you weave."

Athena then tore Arachne's weavings into shreds. She moved to the girl and tapped her with the staff. Arachne's body shrank smaller and smaller and smaller. As the crowd watched, Arachne turned into a spider.

Arachne scurried to a building nearby. She climbed up the doorway and began to weave a web.

Athena did not lie. Ever since then, Arachne and her spider children have been famous for their weaving. And every time one of their beautiful patterns is found, it is brushed away without a thought about proud Arachne and her contest with Athena.

THE END

Chief Luther Standing Bear was a member of the Oglala band of Sioux Indians. In this story from his autobiography, the chief tells of his first buffalo hunt, an important event in a young Sioux warrior's life.

My First Buffalo Hunt

adapted from *My Indian Boyhood*

by Chief Luther Standing Bear
illustrated by James Watling

[PART ONE]

I had learned to make arrows and tip them with feathers. I knew how to ride my pony, no matter how fast he would go, and I felt I was brave and did not fear danger. All these things I had learned for just this day when Father would allow me to go with him on a buffalo hunt. It was the day for which every Sioux boy eagerly waited. To ride side by side with the best hunters of the tribe, to hear the terrible noise of the great herds as they ran, and then to help bring home the kill made this the most thrilling day of any Indian boy's life.

We all knew that the scouts had come in and reported buffalo near and that we must all keep the camp in stillness. Even the horses and dogs were quiet, and all night not a horse neighed and not a dog barked. Quiet was everywhere.

The night before a buffalo hunt was always an exciting night, even though it was quiet in camp. There would be much talk in the tipis around the fires. There would be sharpening of arrows and of knives. New bowstrings would be made, and quivers would be filled with arrows.

It was in the fall of the year, and the evenings were cool as Father and I sat by the fire and talked over the hunt. I was only eight years of age, and I knew that my father did not expect me to get a buffalo at all, but only to try perhaps for a small calf should I be able to get close enough to one. I was greatly excited as I sat and watched Father working in his easy, firm way.

You can picture me, I think, as I sat in the glow of the campfire, my little brown body bare to the waist, watching, listening to my father. My hair hung down my back, and I wore moccasins and a breechcloth of buckskin. To my belt was fastened a rawhide holster for my knife, and this night, I remember, I kept it on all night. I went to sleep with my bow in hand to be all the nearer ready in the morning when the start was made.

The next morning the leaders went ahead until they saw the herd of grazing buffalo. Then they stopped and waited for the rest of us to ride up. We all rode slowly up to the herd, which had come together as soon as they saw us. They ran close together, all of them, as if at the command of a leader. We continued riding slowly toward the herd until one of the leaders shouted, "Ho-ka-he!" which means "Ready, go!" At that command every man started for the herd. I had been listening too, and the minute the hunters started, I rode with them.

Away I went, my little pony putting all he had into the race. It was not long before I lost sight of Father, but I kept going just the same. I threw my blanket back, and the chill of the autumn morning struck my body, but I did not mind. On I went. It was wonderful to race over the ground with all these horsemen about me. There was no shouting, no noise of any kind except the pounding of horses' feet. The herd was now running and had raised a cloud of dust. I felt no fear until we had entered this cloud of dust and I could see nothing about me—I could only hear the sound of feet. Where was Father? Where was I going? On I rode through the cloud, for I knew I must keep going.

[PART TWO]

All at once I saw that I was in the midst of the buffalo. Their dark bodies were rushing all about me, and their great heads were moving up and down to the sound of their hoofs beating upon the earth. Then I was afraid, and I leaned close down upon my little pony's body and clutched him tightly. I can never tell you how I felt toward my pony at that moment. All thought of shooting had left my mind. I was filled with fear. In a moment or so, my senses became clearer and I could hear other sounds besides the clatter of feet. I could hear a shot now and then, and I could see the buffalo beginning to break up into small bunches. I could not see my father or any of the others yet, but I was not so frightened any more.

I let my pony run. The buffalo looked too large for me to tackle anyway, so I just kept going. The buffalo became more and more scattered. Pretty soon I saw a young calf that looked about my size. I remembered now what Father had told me the night before as we sat about the fire. Those instructions were important for me to follow now. I wanted to try for that young buffalo calf.

I was still back of the calf, unable to get alongside of him. I was eager to get a shot yet afraid to try. I was still very nervous. While my pony was making all speed to come alongside, I tried a shot, and to my surprise my arrow landed. My second arrow glanced along the back of the animal and sped on between the horns, making only a slight wound.

My third arrow hit a spot that made the running beast slow up. I shot a fourth arrow, and though it, too, landed, it was not a fatal wound. It seemed to me that it was taking a lot of shots, and I was not proud of my marksmanship. I was glad, however, to see the animal going slower, and I knew that one more shot would make me a hunter. My horse seemed to know his own importance. His ears stood straight forward, and it was not necessary for me to urge him to get closer to the buffalo.

I was soon by the side of the buffalo, and one more shot brought the chase to an end. I jumped from my pony and stood by my fallen buffalo. I looked all around wishing that the world could see. But I was alone.

I was wondering what to do when I heard my father's voice calling, "To-ki-i-la-la-hu-wo?" ["Where are you?"] I quickly jumped on my pony and rode to the top of a little hill nearby. Father saw me and came to me at once. He was so pleased to see me and glad to know that I was safe. As he came up, I said as calmly as I could, "Father, I have killed a buffalo." His smile changed to surprise, and he asked me where my buffalo was. I pointed to it, and we rode over to where it lay.

Father set to work to skin it for me. I had watched him do this many times and knew perfectly well how to do it myself, but I could not turn the animal over.

When the hide was off, Father put it on the pony's back with the hair side next to the pony. On this he arranged the meat so it would balance. Then he covered the meat carefully with the rest of the hide so no dust would reach it while we traveled home.

Always when arriving home I would run out to play, for I loved to be with the other boys. But this day I stayed close to the tipi so I could hear the nice things that were said about me. It was soon all over camp that I had killed a buffalo.

My father was so proud that he gave away a fine horse. He called an old man to our tipi to cry out the news to the rest of the people in camp.

That ended my first and last buffalo hunt. It lives only in my memory, for the last days of the buffalo are over.

Betsy has to stay indoors because of a bobsled accident. Now she must find a way to entertain herself and her two friends, Tacy and Tib.

The Pink Stationery

from *Betsy and Tacy Go Downtown*

by Maud Hart Lovelace
illustrated by Kathleen McCord

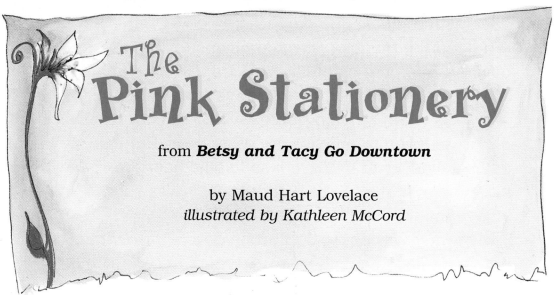

Betsy was out of school for a week, but she didn't mind very much. It was pleasant to snuggle down in bed when she heard the hard-coal heater being shaken down in the morning. Julia and Margaret had to get up; they hurried into their clothes over the open register that brought heat into their bedroom. Betsy didn't need to hurry.

She hobbled downstairs late and spent most of the day on the back-parlor sofa. She liked to watch the red flames flickering behind the isinglass windows of the stove.

After the postcard album came . . . for Jerry sent it! It had leather covers and the seal of Cox School on it . . . she enjoyed putting in her collection of postcards. Postcards from her grandmother in California and from various uncles and aunts, from her father that time he went to St. Paul and from Tib when she went to visit in Milwaukee.

She had two new books to read for she had been to the library just the Saturday before the bobsled party. Miss Sparrow had picked them out for her. *The Water Babies* by Charles Kingsley and *Pickwick Papers* by Charles Dickens.

When she grew tired of reading she played paper dolls.

Betsy hardly ever played with her paper dolls any more. Yet she loved them; she didn't want to throw them away. And when she was sick, or kept indoors for any reason, she got them out and played with them.

At last, however, she grew sick of paper dolls, too.

Her mother was going out that day. She and Margaret were going to the high school to hear Julia sing at the Literary Society program. It was Rena's afternoon off.

"I'm glad Tacy and Tib always come in after school," Mrs. Ray said. "You won't be alone very long."

She put out a plate of cookies to be ready for Tacy and Tib, and she and Margaret kissed Betsy and went out. Old Mag, hitched to the cutter, was waiting in front of the house. Mr. Ray had left her there at noon.

Betsy waved from the back-parlor window, and when the cutter had vanished down Hill Street and the sound of the sleighbells had died, she kept on staring out of doors. The street was empty. There was nothing to see but snow glistening in the sunshine.

Betsy stared a long time. Then she hobbled upstairs to her desk and brought down one of those tablets marked "Ray's Shoe Store. Wear Queen Quality Shoes."

When Tacy and Tib came in after school, they found her on the sofa, scribbling furiously. Her braids had come loose, her cheeks were red, and there was a smudge on her nose.

"I'm just finishing a story," she said. "Would you like to hear it?"

191

"You bet. Swell," said Tacy and Tib.

"It'll be done in a jiff."

Tacy and Tib took off their wraps and stowed them away in the closet. They helped themselves to cookies and sat down in comfortable chairs.

By that time Betsy was ready. She sat up and cleared her throat.

"It's a very good story," she said.

She announced the title sonorously.

"Flossie's Accident."

Betsy liked to read her stories aloud and she read them like an actress. She made her voice low and thrillingly deep. She made it shake with emotion. She laughed mockingly and sobbed wildly when the occasion required.

And she was right about this story. It was a good one. Tacy soon stopped munching cookies and leaned forward in excitement. Tib cried real tears. She always cried real tears in the most flattering manner when Betsy's stories were sad.

Flossie's Accident was very, very sad.

It was about a girl named Flossie who was hurt in a bobsled accident. The accident was something like Betsy's, but Flossie didn't look like Betsy. She had long black ringlets, and big black eyes, and a dead white skin with lips as red as blood. She was dressed all in fluffy white fur, white coat and cap, mittens, boots and everything. She was white as a snowdrift and very beautiful.

When the bobsled turned over, her head was broken off. She was still alive and beautiful, but she didn't have a head.

Her father and mother didn't like the way she looked.

"You are no child of ours," they said, and cruelly shut the door in her face.

Bad boys and girls threw snowballs at her. They laughed at her and chased her.

Holding her head by its long black ringlets, she ran along the frozen river.

"Could she see with it?" Tib interrupted.

"Oh, yes. She could see. She held it up like a lantern."

"Could she hear?"

"Yes. She could hear too. She couldn't eat though. It wouldn't have been practical for her to eat."

"I should think she'd have starved to death," said Tib.

Betsy did not answer.

Flossie followed the river as far as St. Paul. It met the Mississippi there. She followed it to St. Louis, to Memphis, to New Orleans. Forlorn and outcast she wandered everywhere.

She shunned towns and cities, for the people in them laughed at her; or worse still, they ran from her in terror. But after dark she liked to look in at the windows of houses where happy families lived.

Sometimes she saw good things to eat on the tables. Baked beans and brown bread. Or stewed chicken with dumplings. Or pancakes with maple syrup. She looked at them longingly, for she was very hungry.

She saw children romping beside the hard-coal heaters and husbands kissing their wives.

Flossie's heart almost broke when she saw scenes like that. She couldn't ever get married without a head. She couldn't have children. In fact, there was nothing Flossie could do. She couldn't teach school. She couldn't clerk in a store. She couldn't do anything but wander.

So she kept on wandering.

"Did she wear her fur coat all the time?" Tib wanted to know.

"Yes," answered Betsy. "She wore it year in and year out."

"It must have been pretty hot in the summer time."

"Sweltering. There was one good thing about that coat though. It never got dirty. Wherever she went or whatever she did, it stayed as white as snow."

Flossie wandered and wandered, as the story ran on and on. Her adventures were many and excruciatingly sad. At last she hid in a ship and crossed the ocean. When she got off, she was in Greece.

She was walking along a road there (carrying her head, of course), when she met a handsome youth. He had blond hair and blue eyes and tanned rosy cheeks.

"He reminds me of Herbert Humphreys," said Tib.

"His name," said Betsy, "was Chauncey."

197

Chauncey did not laugh and jeer at Flossie as other people did. He stopped and asked her kindly what her trouble was.

"You look like the *Winged Victory,*" he said.

She did, too, although she did not have wings. Flossie told him her story.

"Come with me," said Chauncey.

Taking her by the hand, he led her to the top of a mountain. They looked down on olive groves and the blue Mediterranean Sea.

He built a fire of cedar boughs and when smoke began to rise he said a prayer to the gods and goddesses. He was sort of a god himself. He took Flossie's head by its ringlets and swung it back and forth in the smoke from his fire. Then he clapped it on her swanlike neck, and it fastened there at once. She was just as beautiful as she had been before the bobsled accident. They got married and went to live on the Island of Delos, and they had ten children, five boys and five girls.

"That's the end of the story," said Betsy, closing the tablet.

199

"Betsy! It's wonderful!" cried Tacy.

"It's the best story you ever wrote," said Tib.

"It's the best story I ever heard in my life."

"That poor Flossie!"

Tacy jumped to her feet.

"Betsy," she said, excitedly, yet earnestly, "your stories ought to be published. I've been thinking that for a long time although I never mentioned it before."

Betsy looked at Tacy deeply. It was strange, she thought, that Tacy should say that for she had been thinking the very thing herself.

"They're just as good as the stories in the *Ladies' Home Journal*," said Tacy. "Don't you think so, Tib?"

"Better," Tib said.

"How do people get stories published, do you suppose?"

"I think," said Betsy, "they just send them to the magazines."

"Why don't you send this one then?"

"Maybe I will," said Betsy. Her heart leaped up like a little fish in a bowl. "I haven't any good paper though."

"My sister Mary has some," said Tacy. "A box of lovely pink stationery. Got it for her birthday. She'd give me some, I think. And since she isn't at home, I'll just take it."

"You mean . . . right now?"

"Right now. We'll copy that story and get it off."

"I'll print it for you," cried Tib. Tib was famous for her printing.

Tacy seized her coat and overshoes and ran out of the house. Tib opened the bookcase desk and spread Betsy's tablet on it. She took Betsy's pencil out to the kitchen and sharpened it to an exquisite point. Betsy waited, feeling queer inside.

Tacy came back breathless with the pink stationery.

"I didn't dare take more than one sheet. Do you think you can get the story on, Tib?"

"I think so," said Tib. "I'll print small."

She set to work with painstaking care. While she labored, Betsy and Tacy made plans.

"Betsy," said Tacy solemnly, "you're going to be famous after that story is published."

"How much do you suppose I'll be paid for it?" Betsy asked.

"Oh, probably a hundred dollars."

"What shall we spend it for?"

"Let's see! What!"

They decided to buy silk dresses with hats to match. A blue one for Tacy (because she had red hair). A pink one for Betsy and a yellow one for Tib.

"We'll wear them to Mrs. Poppy's party," said Betsy.

"We'll wear them to the next matinee Winona takes us to. They'll look fine in a box," Tacy said.

"See here," said Tib, sounding worried. "It's going to be hard to squeeze this story on."

"Oh, you can squeeze it on," said Betsy.

"I'll have to print awfully small."

"It doesn't matter," said Tacy. "They'll be so anxious to know how that story's coming out that they'll use a microscope on it, if they have to."

So Tib persisted, and by printing very, very, very small she got all the story on the sheet of pink stationery, down to the last word.

Flossie's Accident

Once upon a time there was a beautiful girl named Flossie. She had long, long, black ringlets and white, white skin with beautiful red lips. She was bobsledding one day when her sled turned over and cut off her head. She was still very beautiful but she had no head on her shoulders. She carried it with her everywhere she went everywhere but everywhere she went children laughed at her, and threw snowball at her. Flossie's parents shut the door in her face. Life for Flossie was very sad and very hard. She left home and followed the Mississippi river as far as it went. She only went out at night because people laughed at her if they saw her during the day. She looked into the homes and saw happy families and it made her very sad because she did not think she would ever be happy or have a family. She wore her coat all the time. It never got dirty. Flossie wandered and wandered all over the ocean she hid in a ship that crossed the Mediterranean Sea. and landed in Greece. At last she met a handsome young man named chancey in Greece. He did not laugh or run from her. He prayed to the gods and goddesses to help Flossie. He put Flossie's head back on her. They got married and had ten children. they were happy forever and ever.

"I saw the Lord's Prayer printed on a dime one time," said Betsy. "It looked a good deal like that."

They put the pink stationery into an envelope and addressed it to the *Ladies' Home Journal,* Independence Square, Philadelphia, Pa. Betsy found a stamp and stuck it on.

"I'll put it in the mailbox on my way home," said Tib, sighing with content.

They all sat on the sofa then, while the sky, behind brown tree trunks, took on the tint of mother-of-pearl, matching the tint of the snow. They planned about the silk dresses and hats.

Betsy and Tacy and Tib were twelve years old now, and when they made plans like that they didn't quite believe them. But they liked to make them anyhow.

About the Author

Maud Hart Lovelace was born in 1892 in Mankato, Minnesota. Her hometown and her home state served as inspiration for her writings. She began her career writing historical novels set in Minnesota. She modeled Deep River, Minnesota, the setting of the *Betsy-Tacy* series, after her hometown. The ten *Betsy-Tacy* novels follow the girls from childhood to adulthood. Lovelace used the people and places she knew to create the world of Deep River. She even patterned Betsy, the main character in the series, after herself.

Country Life

*It is only in the country that we can get
to know a person or a book.*
—Cyril Connolly—

Marly and her family have moved to Pennsylvania to live on a farm. This move is a big change for Marly. She learns about getting maple syrup from trees, the beauty of the seasons, and all the miracles nature provides. She also runs across some of the "dangerous" creatures found in the country.

Journey for Meadow Boots

from **Miracles on Maple Hill**

by Virginia Sorensen
illustrated by John Kanzler

Marly's really scary adventure happened during Easter vacation. One day she was on the lumber road back of the house when she saw something new and different that even Mr. Chris hadn't mentioned. Bright yellow. A different flower. It was beyond the old pasture, near the woods. It made her laugh to think of maybe finding a flower Mr. Chris had never met. She walked toward it, along the rail fence that marked the edge of Grandma's land. Rail fences were good to keep, Mr. Chris said, because bushes and little trees and things grew in all the corners, on both sides, and made safe places for building nests—as safe as thornbushes.

Squirrels could run along the fences, too. Marly saw them trotting along the tops as if they thought the fences were their own special little highways.

At the bottom of the hill she saw the yellow flowers over the fence. They looked like puddles of gold in among the cattail leaves. She climbed over the fence and tried to go straight out toward one bunch of flowers. But the ground was all oozy underfoot. She felt with her shoe for a firm grassy place. And another one. And another. Finally she could reach the flowers if she stretched, and began to gather some. They looked just like buttercups now she was close, only bigger, with the same bright shine on their petals. Suddenly she heard something and looked up. It sounded like buffalo running in a herd, just the way they ran in the movies, pounding all together . . . But here, for goodness' sakes, there weren't any buffalo.

Then she saw them coming. Not buffalo. Just cows, young white-faced cows in a great crowd. And they were coming straight for her!

She dropped the flowers and started to make for the fence, but her feet went in. There wasn't time to search for the dry grassy places now. She splashed. Her feet sank at every step. She heard herself cry out and could hear her own breathing. She felt one shoe come off, deep in the mud. And then she stood on a little island of grass, too scared to move another step.

The cows had come pounding up to the very edge of the little swamp. There they brought up suddenly, all together. The ones in back pushed up into the front row to stare at her. They stood looking and looking, the whole big bunch of them, with round, wide eyes.

She stared back at them. They didn't move, except sometimes to toss their heads as if they were angry at her for being in a place where she didn't belong. Did cows object to people who picked their flowers? she wondered. Come to think of it, she had heard of yellow flowers called *cowslips;* maybe this was their special flower.

"Git! Go away!" she cried and waved her arms at them.

They looked at each other in a kind of amazement and then back at her. But they didn't move away. They only moved a little closer.

213

"Git!" she cried, the way she had always done to nippy dogs who chased her on her bicycle. She took one careful step toward the fence, and the whole long row of them began moving again. How in the world was she ever going to get back over that fence? It seemed a mile away, and those cows didn't seem to want her to get there. The ends of the row moved in a little, so she stood in the center of their wide half-circle. Their eyes were like footlights, and she was right in the very middle of the stage.

Another careful step, and they all moved again. One spoke to her in a low voice. "Moooooooooooo!"

She began to talk to herself, saying, "They're not mean little cows at all. They're just *curious.*"

But the reason she said it was because she really wasn't sure. They could just close in, if they wanted to, and tramp her under. Nobody would ever know where she had disappeared. Great, long shivers began to go over her from her head to her heels. Oh, Joe! she thought. If only he were here now! Once Joe had been with her when a cow came running over a field, and he just stood still and faced her, as brave as could be. And she stopped and mooed at him. He said, "I'll keep her interested while you get away, Marly." And he did. When she was over the fence, she turned around to see what he'd do to escape himself, and he had walked right straight up to that cow and was rubbing her long nose!

She would as soon have touched a lion.

But these cows were lots littler than that other one. They weren't much more than calves, she knew. But there were so many of them, and whatever one did, all the rest hurried to do it, too. One shook its head, and so did all the others. One took a step, and every single one of them took a step.

She tried another hummock. It was firm under her foot. But every cow moved as she took that one step. She could practically feel them breathing. How huge and steady and unblinking were their eyes!

I'll never go anywhere without Joe again, she thought, or without Mother, or Daddy, or Mr. Chris.

Then the horrible thought came that maybe she would never go anywhere again at all, with or without anybody. All the rest of time she would just be stuck in this terrible swamp . . .

"Git! Go away!" she cried again, and shook both her arms at them.

"Mooooo!" one said, and lifted its nose as it spoke as if making a signal to somebody far off. It tossed its head. Every cow in the circle tossed its head then and said "Mooooo!" It was terrible.

"Please let me get to the fence. Let me get to the fence," Marly whispered to herself, like a prayer, and looked carefully at every green spot between her and the beautiful rails where a squirrel was running, stopping to watch her a minute then trotting on again. If she jumped quickly there—and there—and if she didn't slip and fall—then she would be at the fence.

She had to try. There was nothing else to do.

She took a deep breath and looked straight at the cows and spoke in a low voice as friendly (and shaky) as it could be. "My name is Marline," she said, "but everybody calls me Marly. Do you belong to Mr. Chris? I'll bet you're Mr. Chris's cows, aren't you? I heard him telling Mother how many nice calves he had." They looked very interested. Some of them glanced at each other, and one of them actually nodded. Then they all nodded, the whole row. She took a step.

The whole row moved again.

I've got to—*I've got to* . . . Help me get to that fence. And she turned quickly and made one big leap, and another, and splashed and sank and ran through the water and the cattails, and clung to the fence. And then she was up and over.

Instantly the whole bunch of cows were right by the fence, looking at her. But she was safe.

She sat down on the ground, shivering horribly.

And the row of cows looked very pleased, really, and satisfied just to see what she meant to do next. Now she saw how funny they looked, young and curious and wide-eyed. They were exactly like a row of children looking over the fences at the zoo. She smiled at them, knowing they couldn't get over that fence. She was rather surprised when they didn't smile back.

All the time she crossed the field, they stood watching her. She could tell how wonderful and interesting they thought she was, all muddy and barefoot, and now she really knew they hadn't meant to worry her. They were just full of pushing, too, and they would have been sorry if they had pushed her into that swamp and lost her in the mud. She could see now how it had been. They had heard somebody strange splashing around in their drinking place and had to find out who it was.

Now she could laugh.

When she told the family at supper, everybody laughed. But Mother said it was a shame to lose her shoes, even though they were old ones. When she told Mr. Chris the next day, he said he'd take her over and introduce her to those cows properly, which he did. With him there she didn't mind facing the whole circle of them, although she did hang onto Mr. Chris's big hand.

The odd thing was that Mr. Chris said her adventure had probably saved the lives of every single calf! He should have known enough to fence that swamp off before this, he said, with an electric wire. Once he had a herd go in and eat those very flowers she was after. They were called cowslips sometimes, and sometimes marsh marigold. If cows ate too many, their stomachs swelled, and sometimes they died before the doctor could come to help.

What wonderful names he knew for *that* flower! Some called them "capers" and some called them "meadow boots." And when he was a boy, his mother had called them "crazy bet."

"*I'm* going to call them 'meadow boots,'" Marly said. "That's what they need where they grow."

After the wire was up, she and Mother went back for a nice bouquet and some supper greens. The leaves made fine greens, Mr. Chris said, before the spinach was ready. The cows came thundering toward Marly and Mother just the way they had before, but 'way back they stopped like magic. It didn't take them long to learn where the electric fence was strung. They looked a little sad, she thought, not to be able to come close enough to see what she was doing.

About the Author

Virginia Sorensen was born in Provo, Utah, in 1912. Her novels, short stories, and children's books earned her the title "Utah's First Lady of Letters." Sorensen received many impressive honors for her writing. For example, *Miracles on Maple Hill* won the Newbery Medal in 1957 as the most distinguished children's book of the year.

Life at Hill Top Farm

from *The Country Artist: A Story about Beatrix Potter*

by David R. Collins
illustrations by Beatrix Potter
from *Beatrix Potter: The Complete Tales*

Beatrix Potter is one of the most beloved children's book authors of all time. Peter Rabbit, the Flopsy Bunnies, and Squirrel Nutkin are just a few of her famous creations. Her earliest books, such as The Tale of Peter Rabbit *and* The Tailor of Gloucester, *were derived from the stories she told the children of her close friends, Annie and Edwin Moore. Her brother, Bertram, and her friend, Millie Warne, were also important influences on her writing. However, it was a special place—not a person—that inspired many of her later stories.*

During the years that followed, Beatrix found herself remembering past summers in the country that had made her feel happy and free. Sheep and cattle grazing in the pastures, sparkling brooks, and meadows of wildflowers all gave her special joy. When a small farm in the Lake District came up for sale in 1905, Beatrix bought it. She was proud that she had earned the money to buy it herself from the sales of her books.

It was called Hill Top Farm.

The main house was a small gray cottage that
looked as though it had sprouted out of the hill
it sat upon. Climbing vines laced
the outside walls. Roses and lilacs
grew wild in the surrounding
garden. Inside there were small
rooms and a big kitchen that had
never had electricity.

"It is my heaven," Beatrix wrote
to Millie Warne.

Hill Top Farm offered an escape
from No. 2 Bolton Gardens.
Whenever she could, Beatrix fled
from the dreariness of London to
the fresh open country. The
creatures of Hill Top inspired her to create many
new story characters. Rats seemed to think the
cottage belonged to them, and their story came to
life in *The Roly-Poly Pudding*. Beatrix portrayed a
friendlier acquaintance in *The Tale of Jemima
Puddle-Duck*. Readers visited her garden in *The
Tale of Tom Kitten* and *The Tale of Pigling Bland*.

Brother Bertram tried to persuade Beatrix to move to Scotland where he now lived. He still drew and painted, but he was a farmer too. Although she appreciated his invitation, Beatrix declined. England was her home. She still felt an obligation to look after Mr. and Mrs. Potter in their later years.

But Beatrix spent time on Hill Top Farm whenever she could. A farmer, John Cannon, stayed there with his family, taking care of things while Beatrix was in London. She had him build special living quarters for himself and his family, a small library for her books and Bertram's paintings, and a dairy.

The animal family at Hill Top grew. Sheep, pigs, cows, and chickens all lived there. John Cannon taught Beatrix about raising livestock. Before long she was showing prize sheep in local fairs. "That ram obeys you as if you were his mother," one sheep judge remarked. Beatrix smiled. A mother was exactly what she felt like!

As Beatrix spent more and more time on the farm, she spent less and less time writing and drawing. There was always a fence to have fixed or a bush to prune. She loved to walk to the village of Sawrey nearby and often returned with garden plants that friendly neighbors had given her to plant at Hill Top.

Yet, when she *did* create, Beatrix depicted the world that was her delight. Ten new books—in nine years—grew out of her life in the country. In them Hill Top Farm appeared often, with its cupboards and attics, its hiding spots in the garden, its lively farmyard of gossiping animal neighbors.

"A writer should use what [she] knows and feels," Beatrix wrote to Millie. "I suppose I shall always be a child. I am afraid my parents would frown on me for making such a statement. Yet perhaps there are a few of the younger set who will understand me. It is for them I write and sketch. I hope I can bring them pleasure."

There was little doubt of that. Children everywhere begged their parents for another reading of the tales of Mr. Jeremy Fisher, the Flopsy Bunnies, or Mrs. Tittlemouse. Each book by Beatrix Potter was an instant success.

As the new books appeared, the earlier titles spread to more bookstores and libraries. Peter Rabbit quickly became a favorite of young readers in France, Germany, and Spain. Beatrix's first story was translated into more and more languages so that children far from England could learn of Peter's adventure. Although the words were different in other languages, the story remained the same and was loved everywhere. The book was brought to America and published there by people who paid Beatrix nothing for the story, but it pleased her to know that American boys and girls welcomed Peter too.

The Homestead Act of 1862 gave people the
chance to own a quarter-section of land (160 acres)
without paying for it. However, the land wasn't
free. To rightfully own the land, a homesteader had
to live on the land and maintain it for five years.

In this selection, Laura Ingalls Wilder deals with
the difficulty of "holding down a claim." Wilder
also shows how important it is to have a good
neighbor and friend on the prairie.

Holding Down a Claim

from *These Happy Golden Years*

by Laura Ingalls Wilder
illustrated by Garth Williams

Uncle Tom went East on the train next
morning. When Laura came home from
school at noon, he was gone.

"No sooner had he gone," said Ma, "than Mrs.
McKee came. She is in distress, Laura, and she
asked me if you would help her out."

"Why, of course I will, if I can," Laura said. "What is it?"

Ma said that, hard as Mrs. McKee had worked at dressmaking all that winter, the McKees could not afford to move to their claim yet. Mr. McKee must keep his job at the lumberyard until they saved money enough to buy tools and seed and stock. He wanted Mrs. McKee to take their little girl, Mattie, and live on the claim that summer, to hold it. Mrs. McKee said she would not live out there on the prairie, all alone, with no one but Mattie; she said they could lose the claim, first.

"I don't know why she is so nervous about it," said Ma. "But it seems she is. It seems that being all alone, miles from anybody, scares her. So, as she told me, Mr. McKee said he would let the claim go. After he went to work, she was thinking it over, and she came to tell me that if you would go with her, she would go hold down the claim. She said she would give you a dollar a week, just to stay with her as one of the family."

"Where is the claim?" Pa inquired.

"It is some little distance north of Manchester," said Ma. Manchester was a new little town, west of De Smet. "Well, do you want to go, Laura?" Pa asked her.

"I guess so," Laura said. "I'll have to miss the rest of school, but I can make that up, and I'd like to go on earning something."

"The McKees are nice folks, and it would be a real accommodation to them, so you may go if you want to," Pa decided.

"It would be a pity, though, for you to miss Mary's visit home," Ma worried.

"Maybe if I just get Mrs. McKee settled on the claim and used to it, I could come home long enough to see Mary," Laura pondered.

"Well, if you want to go, best go," Ma said. "We needn't cross a bridge till we come to it. Likely it will work out all right, somehow."

So the next morning Laura rode with Mrs. McKee and Mattie on the train to Manchester. She had been on the cars once before, when she came west from Plum Creek, so she felt like a seasoned traveler as she followed the brakeman with her satchel, down the aisle to a seat. It was not as though she knew nothing about trains.

It was a seven mile journey to Manchester. There the trainmen unloaded Mrs. McKee's furniture from the boxcar in front of the passenger coach, and a teamster loaded it onto his wagon. Before he had finished, the hotelkeeper was banging his iron triangle with a spike, to call any strangers to dinner. So Mrs. McKee and Laura and Mattie ate dinner in the hotel.

Soon afterward the teamster drove the loaded
wagon to the door, and helped them climb up
to sit on the top of the load, among the rolls of
bedding, the kitchen stove, the table and chairs
and trunk and boxes of provisions. Mrs. McKee
rode in the seat with the teamster.

Sitting with their feet hanging down at the side
of the wagon, Laura and Mattie clung to each
other and to the ropes that bound the load to the
wagon, as the team drew it bumping over the
prairie. There was no road. The wagon wheels
sank into the sod in places where it was soft
from the melting snow, and the wagon and its
load lurched from side to side. But it went very
well until they came to a slough. Here where the
ground was lower, water stood in pools among
the coarse slough grass.

"I don't know about this," the teamster said, looking ahead. "It looks pretty bad. But there's no way around; we'll just have to try it. Maybe we can go across so quick the wagon won't have time to sink down."

As they came nearer to the slough, he said, "Hang on, everybody!"

He picked up his whip and shouted to the horses. They went fast, and faster, till urged on by his shouts and the whip they broke into a run. Water rose up like wings from the jouncing wagon wheels, while Laura hung onto the ropes and to Mattie with all her might.

Then all was quiet. Safe on the other side of the slough, the teamster stopped the horses to rest.

"Well, we made it!" he said. "The wheels just didn't stay in one place long enough to settle through the sod. If a fellow got stuck in there, he'd be stuck for keeps."

It was no wonder that he seemed relieved, for as Laura looked back across the slough she could see no wagon tracks. They were covered with water.

Driving on across the prairie, they came finally to a little new claim shanty, standing alone. About a mile away to the west was another, and far away to the east they could barely see a third.

"This is the place, ma'am," the teamster said. "I'll unload, and then haul you a jag of hay to burn, from that place a mile west. Fellow that had it last summer, quit and went back East, but I see he left some haystacks there."

He unloaded the wagon into the shanty, and set up the cook-stove. Then he drove away to get the hay.

A partition cut the shanty into two tiny rooms. Mrs. McKee and Laura set up a bedstead in the room with the cook-stove, and another in the other room. With the table, four small wooden chairs, and the trunk, they filled the little house.

"I'm glad I didn't bring anything more," said Mrs. McKee.

"Yes, as Ma would say, enough is as good as a feast," Laura agreed.

The teamster came with a load of hay, then drove away toward Manchester. Now there were the two straw-ticks to fill with hay, the beds to make, and dishes to be unpacked. Then Laura twisted hay into sticks, from the little stack behind the shanty, and Mattie carried it in to keep the fire going while Mrs. McKee cooked supper. Mrs. McKee did not know how to twist hay, but Laura had learned during the Hard Winter.

As twilight came over the prairie, coyotes began to howl and Mrs. McKee locked the door and saw that the windows were fastened.

"I don't know why the law makes us do this," she said. "What earthly good it does, to make a woman stay on a claim all summer."

"It's a bet, Pa says," Laura answered. "The government bets a man a quarter-section of land, that he can't stay on it five years without starving to death."

"Nobody could," said Mrs. McKee. "Whoever makes these laws ought to know that a man that's got enough money to farm, has got enough to buy a farm. If he hasn't got money, he's got to earn it, so why do they make a law that he's got to stay on a claim, when he can't? All it means is, his wife and family have got to sit idle on it, seven months of the year. I could be earning something, dressmaking, to help buy tools and seeds, if somebody didn't have to sit on this claim. I declare to goodness, I don't know but sometimes I believe in woman's rights. If women were voting and making laws, I believe they'd have better sense. Is that wolves?"

"No," Laura said. "It's only coyotes, they won't hurt anybody."

They were all so tired that they did not light
the lamp, but went to bed, Laura and Mattie in
the kitchen and Mrs. McKee in the front room.
When everyone was quiet, the loneliness seemed
to come into the shanty. Laura was not afraid,
but never before had she been in such a lonely
place without Pa and Ma and her sisters. The
coyotes were far away, and farther. Then they
were gone. The slough was so far away that the
frogs could not be heard. There was no sound
but the whispering of the prairie wind to break
the silence.

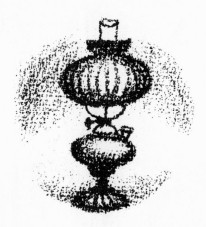

About the Author

Laura Ingalls Wilder was born in 1867 in a United States that was changing rapidly due to westward expansion. In her novels, Wilder was able to capture much of the pioneer spirit of the times as well as the day-to-day existence on the prairie.

Wilder is best known for her *Little House* book series. She wrote and published the first of these books when she was sixty-five. *These Happy Golden Years* is the last book in the series.

Glossary

Pronunciation Key

a as in **at**	**o** as in **ox**	**ou** as in **out**	**ch** as in **chair**
ā as in **late**	**ō** as in **rose**	**u** as in **up**	**hw** as in **which**
â as in **care**	**ô** as in **bought** and **raw**	**ū** as in **use**	**ng** as in **ring**
ä as in **father**		**ûr** as in **turn, germ, learn, firm, work**	**sh** as in **shop**
e as in **set**	**oi** as in **coin**		**th** as in **thin**
ē as in **me**	**o͞o** as in **book**		**t͟h** as in **there**
i as in **it**	**o͞o** as in **too**	**ə** as in **about, chicken, pencil, cannon, circus**	**zh** as in **treasure**
ī as in **kite**	**or** as in **form**		

The mark (´) is placed after a syllable with a heavy accent, as in **chicken** (chik´ ən).

The mark (´) after a syllable shows a lighter accent, as in **disappear** (dis´ ə pēr ´).

A

acquaintance (ə kwān´ təns) *n.* A person whom one knows but who is not a close friend.

advertise (ad´ vər tīz´) *v.* To make a product better known.

ambergris (am´ bər gris) *n.* A waxy substance, formed in the intestines of sperm whales, used in perfume.

asbestos (as bes´ təs) *n.* Any of several minerals once used as fireproof insulating materials.

B

baffle (baf´ əl) *v.* To confuse or puzzle.

bank (bangk) *n.* The sloped ground along the edge of a body of water.

bewilder (bi wil´ dər) *v.* To confuse completely.

bill (bil) *v.* The act of a bird rubbing its bill against another bird's bill.

boast (bōst) *v.* To speak with too much pride.

bough (bou) *n.* A large branch of a tree.

bound (bound) *v.* To leap about.

bracken (brak´ ən) *n.* A large fern with big, triangular leaves, or fronds.

breechcloth (brēch´ klôth´) *n.* A cloth worn around the lower stomach and hip area.

buckskin (buk´ skin´) *n.* The skin of a male deer or antelope.

bustle (bus´ əl) *n.* Noisy and excited activity.

buttercup (but´ ər kup´) *n.* A type of herb with yellow or white flowers.

bygone (bī´ gon´) *adj.* In the past.

cable car (kā´ bəl kär´) *n.* A car drawn along tracks by a cable.

cattail (kat´ tāl´) *n.* A tall plant with brown fur-like spikes, found in marsh areas.

chitter (chit´ ər) *v.* To make short, sharp sounds.

clammy (klam´ ē) *adj.* Slightly damp and cold. [Middle English, probably from *clammen*, "to smear, stick."]

clatter (klat´ ər) *n.* A noisy banging and rattling sound.

coarse (kôrs) *adj.* Thick and rough.

complicated (kom´ pli kā´ tid) *adj.* Difficult to understand.

conclude (kən klo͞od´) *v.* To reach an end.

conscience (kon´ shəns) *n.* A sense of understanding what is right and what is wrong.

cowslip (kou´ slip´) *n.* A primrose with scented yellow flowers.

cozy (kō´ zē) *adj.* Warm and comfortable.

custom (kus´ təm) *n.* A common, repeated practice.

cutter (kut´ ər) *n.* A small, light sleigh.

> **Pronunciation Key: a**t; l**ā**te; c**â**re; f**ä**ther; s**e**t; m**ē**; **i**t; k**ī**te; **o**x; r**ō**se; **ô** in b**ou**ght; c**oi**n; b**oo**k; t**oo**; f**o**rm; **ou**t; **u**p; **ū**se; t**û**rn; **ə** sound in **a**bout, chick**e**n, penc**i**l, cann**o**n, circ**u**s; **ch**air; **hw** in **wh**ich; ri**ng**; **sh**op; **th**in; **th**ere; **zh** in treasure

dingy (din´ jē) *adj*. Dirty and faded.

discard (dis kärd´) *v*. To throw away or get rid of.

dodge (doj) *v*. To move quickly to avoid being caught.

dread (dred) *v*. To feel great fear.

dreariness (drēr´ ē nes) *n*. Dismal or depressing condition.

dusk (dusk) *n*. The time just before nightfall.

earnestly (ûr´ nist lē) *adv*. With sincere feeling.

eavesdrop (ēvz´ drop) *v*. To listen in on a private conversation without anyone knowing.

essential (i sen´ shəl) *adj*. Absolutely necessary.

excruciatingly (ek skroo´ shē ā ting lē) *adv*. With great suffering.

fierce (fērs) *adj*. Violent or intense. [Middle English *fiers*, from Middle French, from Latin *ferus*, "wild, savage."]

footlights (foot´ līts´) *n*. A line of lights placed at the front of a stage floor.

forlorn (fôr lôrn´) *adj*. Lonely or hopeless.

frankincense (frang´ kin sens´) *n*. A resin from Somalia and southern coastal Arabia used in ancient religious ceremonies. [Middle English *fraunk encense*, from Old French *franc ensens*, from *franc*, perhaps meaning "of high quality" + *ensens*, "incense."]

frond (frond) *n*. A large, divided leaf.

frothy (frô´ thē) *adj*. Bubbly or foamy.

glade (glād) *n.* An open space in a wood or forest.

graze (grāz) *v.* To feed on the growing grasses of a field or plain.

haunch (hônch) *n.* The hip and thickest part of the thigh.

herd (hûrd) *n.* A group of wild animals.

herewith (hēr with´) *adv.* Along with this.

holster (hōl´ stər) *n.* A case for carrying a weapon. [Akin to Old English *heolstor,* "cover" and *helan,* "to conceal."]

hummock (hum´ ək) *n.* A low mound of earth.

inquisitive (in kwiz´ i tiv) *adj.* Curious.

intrigue (in trēg´) *v.* To raise one's interest.

jag (jag) *n.* A small load.

jeer (jēr) *v.* To make fun of.

jounce (jouns) *v.* To shake up and down roughly.

lair (lâr) *n.* A place in which a wild animal rests or lives.

lame (lām) *adj.* Having a disabled body part, which makes movement difficult.

livestock (līv´ stok´) *n.* Farm animals raised for use or profit.

longingly (lông´ ing lē) *adv.* With desire or craving.

loom (lo͞om) *n.* A machine that weaves thread into cloth.

lurch (lûrch) *n.* A sudden jerking motion.

lute (lo͞ot) *n.* A pear-shaped, stringed instrument, similar to a guitar.

majestic (mə jes´ tik) *adj.* Showing greatness.

Pronunciation Key: **a**t; l**ā**te; c**â**re;
f**ä**ther; s**e**t; m**ē**; **i**t; k**ī**te; **o**x; r**ō**se; **ô** in
b**o**ught; c**oi**n; b**oo**k; t**oo**; f**o**rm; **ou**t;
up; **ū**se; t**û**rn; **ə** sound in **a**bout,
chick**e**n, penc**i**l, cann**o**n, circ**u**s; **ch**air;
hw in **wh**ich; ri**ng**; **sh**op; **th**in; **th**ere;
zh in trea**s**ure

marksmanship
(märks′ mən ship′) *n.* Skill in shooting at a target.

melancholy (mel′ ən kol′ ē) *adj.* Depressed or sad.

miser (mī′ zər) *n.* A mean person who is stingy with money. [Latin *miser,* "miserable."]

moccasin (mok′ ə sin) *n.* Soft leather shoe or boot without a heel in which the sole is wrapped over the toes and stitched on top.

mockingly (mok′ ing lē) *adv.* With open dislike or with the intention of making fun.

monotonous (mə not′ ə nəs) *adj.* Boringly unchanging. [Greek *monotonos,* from *mon,* "one" + *tonos,* "tone."]

motley (mot′ lē) *n.* A multicolored woolen fabric.

mournfully (môrn′ fəl lē) *adv.* With sorrow.

myrrh (mûr) *n.* A gum resin with a bitter taste, used in incense and perfume, from eastern Africa and Arabia.

neglect (ni glekt′) *v.* To fail to take proper care of.

nightshade (nīt′ shād′) *n.* A poisonous plant related to the tomato and the potato.

nippy (nip′ ē) *adj.* Likely to bite.

nymph (nimf) *n.* Any of the minor spirits or goddesses of classical mythology believed to live in forests, hills, or rivers, and usually represented as beautiful maidens. [Middle English *nimphe,* from Middle French, from Latin *nympha,* "bride."]

object (əb jekt′) *v.* To oppose strongly.

obligation (ob´ li gā´ shən) *n.* A duty or promise to do something.

oozy (oo͞´ zē) *adj.* Slightly liquid and sticky.

parchment (pärch´ mənt) *n.* A material made from treated sheepskin or goatskin prepared for writing on.

partition (pär tish´ ən) *n.* A wall or screen dividing a room.

pasture (pas´ chər) *n.* An area of land used for grazing.

peer (pēr) *v.* To look with curiosity.

persist (pər sist´) *v.* To go on no matter what.

persnickety (pər snik´ i tē) *adj.* Giving overly close attention to small details.

philter (fil´ tər) *n.* A potion that is supposed to have magical power.

pied (pīd) *adj.* Having large spots of different colors.

prairie (prâr´ ē) *n.* A large, flat, grassy area.

propose (prə pōz´) *v.* To set a plan before someone.

protest (prə test´) *v.* To object to something.

provisions (prə vizh´ ənz) *n.* Needed supplies, especially food.

prune (proo͞n) *v.* To cut away unwanted parts of a plant to improve growth or appearance.

queer (kwēr) *adj.* Strange.

quid (kwid) *n.* A bit of chewable substance.

quiver (kwiv´ ər) *n.* A carrying case for arrows.

ragged (rag´ id) *adj.* Torn or worn to shreds.

rampage (ram´ pāj) *v.* To run about wildly.

rawhide (rô´ hīd´) *n.* Cattle skin that has not been made into leather.

Pronunciation Key: a**t**; l**ā**te; c**â**re; f**ä**ther; s**e**t; m**ē**; **i**t; k**ī**te; **o**x; r**ō**se; **ô** in b**ou**ght; c**oi**n; b**oo**k; t**oo**; f**or**m; **ou**t; **u**p; **ū**se; t**û**rn; **ə** sound in **a**bout, chick**e**n, penc**i**l, cann**o**n, circ**u**s; **ch**air; **hw** in **wh**ich; ri**ng**; **sh**op; **th**in; **th**ere; **zh** in trea**s**ure

---

reflection (ri flek´ shən) *n.* Thoughts about a subject matter or idea.

refuge (ref´ ūj) *n.* Safe shelter from something harmful.

ringlet (ring´ lit) *n.* A curly strand of hair.

romp (romp) *v.* To run around or play in a carefree way.

satchel (sach´ əl) *n.* A small bag.

scarab (skar´ əb) *n.* A beetle used in ancient Egypt as a charm.

scrounge (skrounj) *v.* To get by scavenging.

scurry (skûr´ ē) *v.* To move at a quick pace.

shabby (shab´ ē) *adj.* Damaged and faded from wear.

shan't (shant) *v.* Contraction for *shall not.*

shanty (shan´ tē) *n.* A crudely built hut or cabin.

sheepishly (shē´ pish lē) *adv.* With embarrassment.

shelter (shel´ tər) *n.* Something that gives protection.

shilling (shil´ ing) *n.* A coin of little worth. [Akin to Old High German *skilling*, "a gold coin."]

shrill (shril) *adj.* High-pitched in sound.

shun (shun) *v.* To avoid on purpose and constantly.

shuttle (shut´ əl) *n.* A device used in weaving thread into cloth.

Sioux (soo) *n.* Native American people originating in central and southeastern North America.

slosh (slosh) *v.* To splash liquid about.

slough (sloo) *n.* A swamp, marsh, or bog.

solemnly (sol´ əm lē) *adv.* In a serious manner.

sonorously (se nôr´ əs lē) *adv.* With resonance. [Akin to Latin *sonus*, "sound."]

sprout (sprout) *v.* To grow or spring up.

stern (stûrn) *adj.* Harsh or severe.

stride (strīd) *v.* To move with long steps.

surfeit (sûr´ fit) *n.* An excess.

sweltering (swel´ tər ing) *adj.* Very hot.

T

tablet (tab´ lit) *n.* A writing pad.

teamster (tēm´ stər) *n.* A person whose job is driving a team of horses.

thicket (thik´ it) *n.* An area dense with shrubs or small trees.

thong (thong) *n.* A strip made of leather or animal hide.

tipi (tē´ pē´) *n.* A conical tent used by the Native North Americans of the Plains.

titter (tit´ ər) *v.* To giggle.

tramp (tramp) *v.* To walk or step heavily.

transaction (tran zak´ shən) *n.* Exchange or transfer of goods.

tremble (trem´ bəl) *v.* To shiver, or shake involuntarily, with cold or fear.

trilling (tril´ ing) *adj.* Trembling or quavering.

trod (trod) *v.* Stepped or walked on; past tense of *tread.*

trot (trot) *v.* To go in a hurry.

troupe (tro͞op) *n.* A group of traveling actors or entertainers.

tucker (tuk´ ər) *v.* To become very tired; used especially with *out.*

tuffet (tuf´ it) *n.* A clump of grasses or plants.

Pronunciation Key: a̱t; lāte; câre; fäther; set; mē; it; kīte; ox; rōse; ô in bought; coin; bo͞ok; to͞o; form; out; up; ūse; tûrn; ə sound in about, chicken, pencil, cannon, circus; chair; hw in which; ring; shop; thin; there; zh in treasure

unguent (ung´ gwənt) *n.* A soothing ointment.

whereupon (hwâr´ ə pon´) *conj.* Closely following.

whisk (hwisk) *v.* To move quickly.

wistful (wist´ fəl) *adj.* Sadly desiring something.

wolfbane (wo͞olf´ bān´) *n.* A poisonous European herb with yellow or purplish-blue flowers.

⊹ *Cover Credits* ⊱

Illustrated by Mary Collier

⊹ *Unit Opener Acknowledgments* ⊱

Unit 1 illustrated by Deborah Chabrian; **Unit 2** illustrated by Mauro Evangelista; **Unit 3** illustrated by Edward Gazsi; **Unit 4** illustrated by Liz Wolf; **Unit 5** illustrated by Carol Heyer; **Unit 6** illustrated by Anthony Carnabuci

⊹ *Photo Credits* ⊱

13, Alan S. Orling; **31,** ©Bettmann/CORBIS; **63,** ©Marcia Johnson; **77,** file photo; **81,** ©Bettmann/CORBIS; **123,** ©Bettmann/CORBIS; **135,** ©Susan Kuklin/Greenwillow/HarperCollins; **149,** file photo; **161,** ©Frederik Ludwig Storch/Archivo Iconografico, S.A./CORBIS; **207,** Minnesota Historical Society; **221,** ©Jim Theologos/Special Collections, J. Willard Marriott Library, University of Utah; **241,** ©Bettmann/CORBIS.